The
Future
You

The
Future
You

Break Through the Fear
and Build the Life You Want

Brian David Johnson

HarperOne
An Imprint of HarperCollins*Publishers*

HarperCollins books may be purchased for educational, business, or sales promotional use. For information, please email the Special Markets Department at SPsales@harpercollins.com.

FIRST EDITION

Designed by SBI Book Arts, LLC

Library of Congress Cataloging-in-Publication Data

Names: Johnson, Brian David, author.
Title: Future you : break through the fear and build the life you want / Brian David Johnson.
Description: First edition. | San Francisco : HarperOne, 2021
Identifiers: LCCN   2020027751 (print) | LCCN 2020027752 (ebook) |
   ISBN 9780062965066   (hardcover) | ISBN 9780062965073 (trade paperback) |
   ISBN 9780062965080 (ebook)
Subjects: LCSH: Change (Psychology) | Self-realization. | Future, The.
Classification: LCC BF637.C4 J636 2021 (print) | LCC BF637.C4 (ebook) |
   DDC 158.1—dc23
LC record available at https://lccn.loc.gov/2020027751
LC ebook record available at https://lccn.loc.gov/2020027752

21 22 23 24 25   LSC   10 9 8 7 6 5 4 3 2 1

For those who choose the future over fear

CONTENTS

Contents

The
Future
You

CHAPTER 1

Finding the Future You, or Why a Futurist Decided to Write a Self-Help Book

A Tale of Two Phone Calls

No one wakes up one morning and thinks: *I need to see a futurist.* I get called in when dark clouds are forming on the horizon and a company or organization needs help figuring out its next moves.

If you're reading this book, I hope your situation isn't too dire, but you obviously need some advice about your future, maybe as it relates to your job or financial security, or to anxieties around technology, politics, or the economy. Maybe you're worried about how your relationships will play out with your kids or parents. Or there are the big future fears: pandemic, war, sickness, and, of course the mother of them all, death.

I can help. I can't tell you your future, but I can show you how I've helped many people realize theirs, including the specific steps they needed to take to move toward the future they wanted—or at least feel a little better about where they're headed, a little more in control.

Taking that first step is the hardest part. But trust me when I say, you can do it. I'm not saying it will be easy. But I am saying you can do it.

Being worried about the future is just that—worry. Think about how much time and energy you spend worrying about stuff that hasn't happened, and maybe never even will. What if you instead put all that energy toward the creation of a positive and lasting future?

I get it. Even after working as a futurist for a long, long time, I still get worried sometimes, and that's a big reason why I decided to write this book. To show you what I mean, let me tell you about two of the harder phone conversations I've had recently.

Call 1: The CEO in Crisis

It was late. I was reading. My phone buzzed. I recognized the name immediately.

"Hello?" I said.

"This isn't going to work, BDJ," Carol replied quickly, using the nickname most people eventually get to with me. No hello, no pleasantries, just panic and a tightness in her voice. "This isn't the future I want."

"What's wrong? What's going on?" I asked. I kept my voice calm even though I was feeling a tad nervous myself. Carol didn't sound good, and it worried me.

"I don't think I can turn down this client. The opportunity just came in today, and I know we talked about a shift in strategy and I know we said that might mean saying no at times, but . . ." She paused and took a breath. "I know we don't want to do work like this anymore and the firm needs to change direction, but it's nearly three million dollars."

"What did the others on the leadership team say?" I asked.

"I haven't told them yet," she answered. "I'm sitting here trying to think about what to do. This is the future of the firm, the future of my business."

Carol was the CEO of a midsize talent agency in Los Angeles. Ten months ago she and the rest of the leadership team had brought me in to work with them. They were concerned that their firm wasn't prepared for the future, and it was my job to work with them on charting a new path.

We did it. It was a good plan with specific steps, one that would embrace a new generation of talent and influencers, drawn from the emerging social media side of entertainment. That meant changing the types of clients they took on in a pretty sizable way. I won't bore you with the details, but as part of the risk assessment, we had talked about the possibility of a big talent, a traditional

TV star, wanting to join the agency and how that would be hard to turn down.

That time had come, and Carol was scared. I could hear it in her voice. She was worried she wasn't making the right decisions, that she was going to mess up her future, as well as the future of the firm and all the people who worked there.

"You sound frustrated," I said.

"That's because I am!" she snapped. "There are people's lives and jobs here on the line. Not to mention my own family. I'm sorry. I didn't mean to be short with you. What should I do, BDJ? You're the futurist."

I hesitated, suddenly unsure myself. Was she doing the right thing? Who turns down three million dollars? Is that crazy?

"Are you there?" she asked.

I had been silent for too long. It had become uncomfortable, but I didn't know what to say. I was scared too. Here I was, the futurist, and I was suddenly unsure about the future.

The reason I had paused is because something in Carol's voice reminded me of a call I'd taken a few weeks earlier.

Call 2: The College Grad at a Crossroads

I had been walking back from an appointment when Bruno's name popped up on my buzzing phone.

"Hey there," I said.

"I'm a coward," Bruno said, his voice low with dread.

"What's wrong?" I asked. "What happened?"

"Nothing happened," he answered. "That's just it. I couldn't do it."

Bruno was a friend of a friend. He was twenty-two, just out of college. He had a decent enough job but not one with a lot of satisfaction or growth opportunity. He liked where he lived but didn't love it. And he was lonely. A recent breakup with a boyfriend had not gone well. Bruno was having a tough time.

"I locked up in the interview," Bruno explained. "I started worrying that my current manager was going to find out and that I'd get fired. If I get fired, I won't have health insurance, and what if I get sick? What would I do then?"

I paused. It wasn't Bruno's words that made me hesitate. It was the sound of his voice. He was panicked and in distress. The whole point of our conversations over the last few weeks had been to empower him, to give him the confidence needed to go after the future he wanted.

Had I done him harm? Would my advice put him out of a job? It would be crushing if he lost his health insurance. I knew he had some serious underlying health conditions that if left untreated would mean even more trouble.

"Are you still there? Did I lose you?" Bruno asked.

"No, I'm still here . . ." I said, my voice trailing off, the same way it would with Carol a few weeks later.

• • •

The calls with Bruno and Carol made me question myself. What business did I have giving people advice? I don't care if it's about three million dollars or deciding on a career path. What made me think that I could hand out advice?

And then I told myself what I tell myself every time anxiety creeps in: *You can help because you've done it before.* For a quarter century now I've been helping large international corporations, Silicon Valley tech companies, nonprofits, universities, and even governments and militaries figure out their way forward.

Now I want to help you.

Thinking about the future creates a kind of life paralysis. You freeze up. You can't make moves even in your head. You feel like you aren't in control. You get frustrated. You give up.

How can you change your future? There is a process and I can teach it to you, the same way I did with Carol and Bruno. Despite the intense moment of panic (theirs and mine), they did make it to their future. In both cases they ended up taking a break, regrouping, and making sure they felt comfortable with their new direction. Then they started back on the path, what I like to call the path to the Future You.

Finding Future You

Whenever I first meet with a person who is struggling over their future, I talk about the three versions of self that make up every one of us: Past You, Present You, and Future You.

Past You is your experience and memories—your joys and regrets, your victories and defeats, the sum total of your many lessons learned.

Future You is the person you will become. It's who you want to be and also who you don't want to be (much more on this to come).

Then there's Present You.

For most of us, Present You is Past You. We spend our lives in the past. As George Orwell put it, "Who controls the past controls the future: who controls the present controls the past."[*] We don't just remember the past, we are ruled by it, regretting bad decisions and opportunities missed, or looking for ways to forget the bad times. Of course the past isn't all bad (at least I hope not!). There are positive memories and moments of joy.

But whether our past is happy or sad, we spend our lives locked in it. That's why, for most of us, Present You is really Past You.

The problem with this paradigm is that the past is, well, in the past. Short of a total revisionist reinvention of self, there's no way to alter it. It reminds me of another common saying: "People don't change, they only become more so." In a world where Present You is Past You, that inevitably holds true.

But what if you could turn the formula on its head and make Present You into Future You? In that scenario, the person you want to become would be the person you are, and the capacity for change would be limitless.

---

[*] George Orwell, *1984* (London: Secker & Warburg, 1949).

I wrote this book to help you do just this: flip the script and transform Present You into the best version of Future You. I'm excited to give you all the necessary strategies and tools, along with stories of others who learned to embrace their future selves. By the time you reach the end of the book, I promise you will understand your Future You better than ever. Not only that but you will be able to see yourself in the future you want and know the steps you need to take to get there.

You will be your Future You. The journey starts right now.

Okay, but What Exactly Is a Futurist?

I travel a lot for work, often flying halfway around the world. On international flights, I always enjoy filling out the immigration form the flight attendants hand out before landing. In the box asking for my occupation, I like to write in big block letters: "FUTURIST." It's made for some interesting encounters with border control agents, including the big, burly guard at London Heathrow who at first didn't believe my job was for real but by the end couldn't stop asking questions about it, to my increasing consternation, given the enormous queue of travelers waiting behind me. "Well, Mister Futurist," the officer said, finally stamping my passport after what felt like an eternity, "you've got a very interesting job." Then he added, "If you're working on the future, do us a favor and make sure it's a good one."

For most of the past decade, I was the chief futurist at Intel Corporation, the world's leading manufacturer of microprocessors, the chips that power our many computers and devices. Basically, they make the brains that make the electronics. I was the first futurist ever appointed at the company and proud of the work I did. That's why instead of writing "engineer" on my immigration forms, it always gives me great joy to write "FUTURIST."

Through my private practice, my work today involves helping companies and organizations of all sizes look ten to fifteen years into the future to explore possible positive and negative futures. Then I show them how to turn around and look backward to figure out what they need to do today, tomorrow, and five years down the line to move toward a positive future and away from a negative one.

My clients are across industries, including the tech sector, manufacturing, retail, medicine, agriculture, finance, government, and the military. All of these bodies have one thing in common: they all need to make decisions today that might not pay off for many years. It could be an investment decision that will cut into that year's bottom line or the development of a new product that will take a long time to pay dividends.

To make these hard decisions, they need someone who is trained at gathering information and systematically modeling possible futures. That's where futurists come in. As I like to tell my students, "If not us, who?"

My work with clients involves a process called "futurecasting," which I'll get into later in the book. In short, the process relies on a mix of inputs, like social science, technical research, cultural history, economics, trend data, and interviews of experts. I use these various data inputs to determine not only what is probable but also what is possible. That's the great part about being a futurist—showing people what the future may hold.

A few years ago I was brought in by an architecture firm to help them unpack the future of their organization. The firm was more than one hundred years old, and the partners were worried that they weren't well prepared for the future. We got the entire firm together and considered their potential futures. They primarily designed and built educational buildings in the Midwest. But instead of looking just at the future of the firm, we went bigger, exploring the future of education so they could imagine where they wanted to fit in.

That's when something unexpected happened. Yes, they saw the future of their organization, but they also began to understand how education itself needed changing. They saw how they could help shape the future of learning, preparing all learners throughout their lives to thrive in the twenty-first century. They were so inspired that they started a separate nonprofit institute called 9 Billion Schools. Their manifesto:

> The 9 Billion Schools movement was conceived to inspire
> discussion, innovation, and action to help create a world
> where everyone benefits from learning that is personalized
> as well as life-long, life-wide, and life-deep (L3).

> We seek to partner, ideate, and innovate with other
> organizations and individuals who are committed to
> helping realize the 9 Billion Schools vision in ways both
> large and small.*

They were inspired and driven by the possibility of the future and the impact they could have.

As that example shows, my work isn't just about imagining possible futures. I also help clients achieve their best future. That makes me what's known in the industry as an applied futurist. When I first meet people, they like to imagine that I sit around all day with my feet propped up on my desk imagining what the future could be. That couldn't be further from the truth. I'm an engineer and a designer by training. As an applied futurist, I not only chart out these potential futures but also work very closely with people to figure out what steps they need to take. What do they need to do on Monday to move toward the future they desire?

This might mean working closely with a company's human resources department to determine the right hire in the future. Or working with the folks in finance to explore what investments need to be made. I even work with facilities managers to figure out what an office building will need to support its future employees.

---

*"The Philosophy: Our Manifesto," 9 Billion Schools, accessed June 9, 2020, https://9billionschools.org/thephilosophy.

Ultimately, my success as a futurist is measured by giving my clients not only well-researched future scenarios but also pragmatic steps they can take today to get there.

So Why Did This Futurist Decide to Write a Self-Help Book?

Here's the honest truth: Never in a million years did I think you'd be reading this. Even for a guy whose job it is to look out into the future, I never imagined my own future would involve writing a self-help book.

As I've explained, I've been a futurist now for twenty-five years, helping organizations peer into the future and model positive and negative outcomes. Then I work with those same organizations to realize the positive futures and avoid the negative ones. Along with being an engineer and designer by training, I'm also a university professor and science fiction author.

So what am I doing writing a self-help book? That calls for another story . . .

I was fortunate during my time at Intel to have a mentor named Andy Bryant. Andy is a big, approachable guy with a scruffy beard and a passion for golf that borders on obsessional. He served as CFO for many years before being appointed chairman of the board. To understand the kind of guy Andy is, I would often see him commuting back and forth between Oregon, where we both lived at the time, and Santa Clara, California, where Intel has its headquarters. It wouldn't be uncommon to run into Andy sitting in coach, squeezed into a middle seat near the back of a Southwest Airlines 737. Here's the chairman of the board at a two-hundred-billion-dollar-a-year company and he's back in steerage with the rest of us, happy as a clam on his commute to work.

In one of my last mentoring sessions with Andy, he asked me why I had joined Intel in the first place. Before coming to the company, I'd been a designer of interactive television set-top boxes for a small firm. This was the *early* days of the internet, when you had to plug a phone line into the back of your cable box to communicate with the cable company. In other words, a very long time ago.

When I was offered the job at Intel, I was thrilled because it would enable me to work at a global scale. Intel measured its output in the billions of microprocessors. I wanted to fundamentally change the way the company imagined, designed, and built its chips. I wanted to create technology that was centered around people. I wanted my fellow engineers to understand not just that they were making really fast computers but that those really fast computers had the power to change people's lives—and hopefully for the better.

When I told Andy this, he smiled and said, "Well, obviously you didn't set the bar high enough. Because you've accomplished that in the decade you've been with us. Now, what's your next goal?"

After the meeting, I didn't go straight back to my work cubicle. I walked around the sprawling corporate campus and thought hard about what Andy had asked me.

I'm a very specific type of futurist, what's known as a technological and applied futurist. Being a technological futurist is what it sounds like. Most of the work I do is centered around technology and how it can influence society for the better. As for the applied part, that means I not only envision possible futures but also work to make these futures come true.

But I'm also a futurist who cares about people. I think everything we do in life begins and ends with people. There might be a bunch of technology and processes and procedures involved along the way, but it always begins and ends with people. A reporter once joked with me that I'm a technological futuristic who cares more about people than about technology. I took that joke as the ultimate compliment. And as I walked around campus that day, pondering my next goal, it led me to the realization that people are my true passion.

The more I thought about this, the more I realized that for my next act in life, I wanted to do for people what I'd spent the last seven years doing for microprocessors. That is, I wanted to fundamentally change the way people imagine, design, and build their lives. I wanted to help them understand that the future isn't fixed; it's constructed every day by the actions of people. I wanted people to embrace the fact that they can build their own future if—and only if—they are willing to be an active participant in it. What they can't do is let the future happen to them or, even worse, let somebody else design their future for them.

That's why this futurist is writing a self-help book. For so many people the future feels like a blind spot, something they can't see and they can't change. But that's not true. You can, and we can start today. Hopefully you're up for the adventure. Because I'm excited to help you imagine, design, and build the future you've always wanted for yourself, your children, and your community. Who knows? If enough of us climb on board, we might even change the future of the world.

A Hands-On Approach

I want this book to be engaging and relevant to as many readers as possible, so it's filled with stories of everyday people I've helped using my process. I also want the book to be practical and interactive. That's where the Quick Questions come in. These are the sections in each chapter where I encourage you to put the book down and grab a pen and paper. I use these Quick Questions with companies and organizations. They are tools and actions to get people thinking and doing. Just as I'm going to ask you to pick up a pen and write or grab your phone and type, I ask the same thing of CEOs and board members of massive corporations.

That might not be what you signed up for when you picked up this book, but I can't emphasize enough how important it is to the process. As you'll hear me say over and over again, getting to the future you is work. When I engage with a new client, I begin with a series of exploratory interviews to understand their specific needs, before moving into an exhaustive research phase. My team and I gather insights from a multitude of perspectives—anthropology, engineering, market research, technology, and maybe even a dash of science fiction, depending on the project. In the end, we might use hundreds, if not thousands, of data points to model different possible futures for the client.

I'm not trying to freak you out. And the research and thinking I ask of you in the Quick Question sections won't involve anywhere near that level of detail. But it is important that you create the necessary headspace to do the effort that true future work requires.

A final word about process: I know everyone works and thinks differently, but I strongly encourage you to pick up a journal or notebook or at the very least a device for the Quick Questions. In my experience (both my own and what I've seen in others), the physical act of putting pen to paper or typing out the words establishes an immediacy and a realness that's harder to achieve if you're answering the questions in your head. It also helps to have all your meditations on the future in one place. You will need to go back to them to review.

Okay, I will take off my professor's cap now. Before I do, though, I want to leave you with one final thought, the same one I give my students at the start of each semester: "The process is the process." That might not make total sense just yet. But I promise you it soon will.

Up Next: Setting the Future Straight

For many people, the future is at once unknowable and also ruled by misconception. It reminds me of the quote often attributed to Mark Twain, "The trouble with the world is not that people know too little; it's that they know so many things that just aren't so." Before you can take charge of your future, you need to move beyond any long-held fallacies. That's where we're headed together in chapter 2, with its not so subtle title, "Everything You've Been Told About the Future Is Wrong."

Everything You've Been Told About the Future Is Wrong

There is a specter haunting this book. It's the same ghost that haunts people when they think about the future. But what people don't realize is that the scary ghost isn't real. It's a fiction, like an old-fashioned black-and-white movie ghoul.

I think back to 2018 and one of the strangest cocktail-hour conversations I've ever had. I was sitting on a rooftop patio in San Francisco, scene of the twenty-fifth anniversary celebration for *WIRED*, the tech magazine. It just so happened that 2018 was also my twenty-fifth year working as a futurist, so their editor had invited me to speak.

"Can I tell you something kind of weird and personal?" the

young woman sitting next to me asked as she peered out over the bay. Her name was Audrey, and we knew each other casually from a recent project we both had worked on for a movie studio.

"Fire away," I told her.

Audrey proceeded to describe in vivid detail a recent dream she'd had about a post-apocalyptic world filled with drones and robots and augmented reality gone horribly amok.

"Sounds like a science fiction movie," I remarked.

"Yes!" she cried, her face lighting up. Then her brow creased as she talked about the dark turn the dream took. Robots with minds of their own. Self-driving cars going off the rails. Her mother showing up (of course!), only it soon became clear it wasn't really her mother (of course again!). At one point in the dream Audrey took off her AR goggles and realized the futuristic city she thought she was in was actually a bombed-out war zone. She even described for me the smell of burning bodies, which I have to say was in stark contrast to the groovy vibe of the rooftop soirée.

"That's a terrifying dream, Audrey," I told her. I was set to speak in a few minutes, so I begged her pardon for having to get up. "But before I go," I added, "let me assure you that your nightmare scenario won't happen because humans won't let it happen. We're the ones in control here. Especially when it comes to technology, humans will remain at the center. Your nightmare was more about losing control as a human and less about the takeover of technology."

Audrey's dream is a great example of the specter haunting this book. She, like so many people, was terrified of powerlessness. That fear was the driving force for her nightmare. Her mom wasn't her mom. The city wasn't the city. The reality she thought she knew wasn't real at all. Some *thing* had altered her reality and it had control over who she met and what she saw. It had the power. In her nightmare, AR was the tool that was altering that reality. This was made even more frightening for her by the fact that AR is a real technology. Ultimately, however, Audrey's dream was about her not having power over her own future.

In this chapter, we're going to take a closer look at the future, to show how this notion of the future—dark, dystopian, fear based—is a charade, like a special effect in the movies. Just as in the movies, when you see the ghoul for what it is, the fear becomes almost laughable.

To help pull the mask back on the future and turn the full power over to you, I now want to zoom in on a few key truths about it.

Truth 1: The Future Is Not Fixed

I want you to close your eyes and imagine the future. What do you see? Maybe you picture yourself as an old person, walking along the beach or through the streets of some faraway city. If you have kids, you might picture them as adults, perhaps with children of their own. Or maybe your mind's eye imagines a cityscape altered by time or an environment ravaged by the effects of climate change. Whatever your vision of the future, the point is, it's a fixed outcome in time. Because that's what you've been conditioned to believe, that time is unfolding into a clearly defined future. Think destiny, or the idea that fate is something predetermined.

You know what I say to that? Fate is for suckers. At best it's a cop-out and at worst it's a lie. That may be how you've been taught to think about the future, but think again.

The purpose of this book is to show you how to imagine, design, and reach the future you want. In the process, I'm also going to help you figure out how to avoid the futures you don't want. For many people the future is a blind spot. They know it's out there, but they feel like they can't see it. I'm here to tell you that you can. You can see the future. The first step in the process is to understand that everything you have been told about the future is wrong. That's a pretty big, sweeping statement, I know, but hang with me and I'll explain.

The way people—especially those with any kind of power or prominence—talk about the future is all wrong. How many times have you heard some cable TV pundit or government official say some version of the following?:

- "In the future, robots will take all of our jobs."

- "By the year X, you won't be allowed to drive your own car. Self-driving cars will be mandated."

- "In the future, insurance agencies will mandate that we all have monitoring chips implanted in our bodies."

As these examples show, when people talk about the future, the language they use is all wrong, as if the future is an end destination. As if it's a place we're all moving toward. But it's not. They talk about the future like it's Des Moines, Iowa, and we're all going there. But we're not. Don't get me wrong, lovely city, I've been there many times, but you get the point.

Just as we think of the future as a specific place, in the same breath we talk about the future as inevitable. You're going to Des Moines, like it or not. Again, this is not true (and again, no disrespect to Des Moines!). There are many possible futures out there.

So the future isn't fixed and we aren't powerless in moving toward it. That prompts the question, what should you do with that information? Short answer: become an active participant in your future. You can't sit back and let the future happen to you. If you don't want to go to Des Moines, don't go to Des Moines. More important, don't let other people define your future for you. That never ends well. You have the power to shape your future. It's up to you to use it.

This can sound like a monumental task. I get it. Most people don't spend their days and nights thinking about the future. Why should they? It's not their job. We're all busy. We all have work or school or family to think about. For most people, just thinking about what to have for dinner is a big enough act of futurism. And that's okay.

The problem is, people are not given the platform or the permission to think about the future. That's where I come in. My wife likes to say that I live my life ten to fifteen years in the future and commute home on the weekends.

So yes, I can help. That's why I wrote this book, and why you're reading it, to come up with a new way to think about the future. I can't tell you your future. Only you can do that. That's why you need to be wary of people who tell you that they know your future.

Only you can know your future. I can help by giving you the right tools. I can show you ways to not only imagine yourself in the future you want but also identify the pragmatic steps needed to get there.

Now you know that the future isn't a fixed destination, that you have the power to move toward a different future. And that prompts another question. Where do you want to go? What is the future you want? To answer that, you need to imagine yourself in your future, to dream a new dream for your tomorrow. And that takes us to our second key truth about the future.

Truth 2: The Future Will Not Look Like a Science Fiction Movie

When people try to imagine their future, they usually use the one thing they have been shown their whole lives that focuses on the subject: science fiction. And why not? It makes perfect sense. We spend our lives looking at images, most of them moving images, of the future. We've seen what space travel will look like (*The Martian, Ad Astra, Gravity*); future cities (*Minority Report, The Hunger Games, The Fifth Element*); self-driving cars (*Total Recall, Transformers*); robots (*I Robot, A.I. Artificial Intelligence, The Terminator*); and machines that are smarter than us (*Her, Ex Machina, 2001: A Space Odyssey*).

Science fiction is a rich and fabulous realm of possibilities for the future. Why shouldn't we dip into it as the raw material when imagining a future of our own? Well, simply put, because it's also completely wrong. Allow me to explain . . .

First off, if you haven't figured it out already, I'm a geek, a huge and unashamed nerd. I love everything science and everything science fiction. As I mentioned previously, I'm also a science fiction writer—my novel *WaR: Wizards and Robots* tells the story of time-traveling cyborgs and a reluctant teen heroine who stands between the bad bots and planet Earth's total annihilation. So yeah, I'm pretty into the genre. I mean, who doesn't love movies where massive thinking machines fight for control of our planet in the major cities across the world, destroying themselves in the process?

Here's the thing, though: when I stopped being a ten-year-old nerd reading science fiction books in the computer lab at school and started being an adult, everything changed. Science fiction is all fun and games, but if we're going to do the real work of thinking about the future, it's important to leave science fiction at the door. The future doesn't work like that. Science fiction is great entertainment, but you shouldn't use it as the basis for your life planning.

To explain this better, let me introduce you to a friend and collaborator who knows a lot about the ways the future gets imagined.

The Lab Where Worlds Collide

The campus of the University of Southern California is in downtown Los Angeles. The school is known for many things, but its film program is probably its biggest claim to fame. George Lucas, Ron Howard, and a long roster of A-list filmmakers plied their craft there, making the school a draw for young filmmakers and storytellers.

My car dropped me off in front of Shrine Auditorium, with its delicately colored windows and Moorish-revival spire. The theater has hosted all the most prestigious awards ceremonies, including the Grammys, the Oscars, and the Emmys. Like so many buildings near and on the USC campus, it's surrounded by towering palm trees that call to mind Hollywood royalty.

Around the corner from the auditorium is the Zemeckis Center for Digital Arts, named for Robert Zemeckis, who directed films like *Back to the Future* and *Forrest Gump*. I went inside to find Alex McDowell, a professor at USC and head of the so-called World Building Media Lab.

I figured if I'm going to talk to you about ways to think about the future, it would make sense to hear from someone whose very job is to tell stories about the future. That's what Alex does. Among his many accomplishments, he designed the world for the Steven Spielberg film *Minority Report* and the 2013 reboot of Superman, *Man of Steel*.

The weather in Southern California is always sunny and pleasant, and this day was no different. I found Alex in his World Building Media Lab, filled with miniature models of space stations, futuristic buildings, and the like, as well as lots and lots of enthusiastic students.

"Hey, BDJ," Alex said, waving me into his office. Alex is from England and has the kind of accent that makes everything he says sound profound and brilliant. Often what he's saying *is* profound and brilliant, but even when he's just telling you where the bathroom is located, it can sound like deep, personal advice.

"I want to talk about imagining the future," I said after the usual exchange of pleasantries.

"Well, you've come to the right place," he said with a laugh. "Imagining the future is precisely what we do here." He gestured toward a nearby workstation, where a group of students were huddled over a model of what looked like an underwater metropolis.

"My sentiments exactly," I said. "That being said, there's a difference between imagining a science fiction movie future and imagining the real future."

"You couldn't be more right," Alex agreed, leaning back in his chair. Over his shoulder I could see palm trees against a back-drop of bright blue sky. "The point of science fiction movies is to tell a good story. That brings in the audiences, which makes the money, which keeps the studio execs happy. Science fiction, like all of Hollywood, is about making money. Fortunately for us, cre-ating thrilling stories is good for business. People like excitement, they crave it."

"The business point is so true," I said. "When people watch movies about the future, they need to remember that what they're watching is entertainment. It was created with the sole purpose of getting people to part with their $13.50, or whatever the going price of a movie ticket is these days."

"Right," Alex said. "And listen, there's nothing wrong with that. That's my job. I work with guys like Spielberg and Fincher and Gilliam to craft incredibly thrilling and, in their own way, believable worlds. The more believable the world is, the more au-diences feel like it's real, that what they're seeing up there on the big screen could actually happen. In the case of *Minority Report*, we went to great lengths talking to scientists and anthropologists and other experts to make sure that the future we created would feel as real as possible. To hook the audience, we needed to con-vince them that our dark vision could come to pass."

"That darkness is important too," I said. "There needs to be conflict and drama in movies to get people to watch them. No one wants to watch a movie where all the characters are perfect and they live in a perfect world and nothing bad ever happens to them."

"That would be an awful movie," Alex said. "Unless it's *The Truman Show*."

"True," I said, laughing. "But seriously, we need to remember that when we watch science fiction movies about the future, they're not only products being sold; they're purposely dark and dystopian because that makes them dramatic, which in turn makes a better movie."

"It does," Alex said, looking out over the lab. "That's what I train students to do here."

"So if people are serious about imagining their future, they should definitely not base it on science fiction movies," I said. "If we all woke up tomorrow morning and we were living in a science fiction movie, living in *Minority Report*, that wouldn't be good."

"That would be a nightmare," Alex agreed.

"Science fiction . . . great for entertainment," I said, "but bad for life planning"

"I never thought about it that way," Alex said, shifting in his chair. "But yes, you're right."

Truth 3: The Future Has a Dirty Little Secret

Okay, let's review. We've established that the future isn't some fixed entity that we're all hurtling toward, like it or not. We also know that the future isn't going to look like a science fiction movie—and that this is a very good thing. What will it look like, then? That takes us to the third and final truth about the future, which I like to call its dirty little secret.

"It's twenty-five years into the future," a booming voice intoned. "You walk out the door into a world transformed." Cue the sound of beating drums.

I was sitting in a darkened auditorium in New Orleans, having come to the Big Easy for a conference on the future of cities. This was the video kicking off the opening ceremony.

I've seen some version of the "vision video," as it's known in the industry, dozens of times. Sponsor companies and show promoters love to produce them to get the crowd excited about the world of tomorrow and show how cutting-edge they are in their long-term strategic thinking.

In case you couldn't tell, I'm not a huge fan of vision videos.

"Self-driving cars will pilot you to work and take the kids to school," the video continued, showing images of attractive people with perfect smiles and mildly futuristic clothing. This usually means bland and monochromatic. I don't understand why everyone thinks that people will not like bright colors or denim in the future.

"Autonomous drones will deliver you packages and medicine . . ." the narrator continued, though to be honest I had stopped listening. It's not that I don't believe the technologies in these videos are coming. It isn't even that I worry they'll negatively affect our lives and cities.

My problem with these shiny, high-production vision videos is that they try to paper over the dirty little secret about the future.

When people talk about the future, not only do they get it wrong by thinking it's a fixed destination from which we are powerless to deviate. They also make the mistake of talking about the future in terms of sweeping, seismic change.

Here's the dirty little secret about the future: *it's going to look a lot like today.* If you were to go to New York City and take a picture of Fifth Avenue and then compare it to pictures taken from the same spot ten, twenty, even thirty years in the past, you'd see that over the years it has looked pretty much the same. Sure, the cars are different, and the way people dress. But the general look and feel of the place is pretty much the same.

And this is a good thing! Because, as it happens, civilizations don't do well with huge, seismic change. As Alex said, if we were to wake up tomorrow morning and find ourselves living in a science fiction movie, that would be a nightmare.

Plus, if the future is going to look pretty much like today, that means there are just a few specific things you need to learn about how things will change. We'll explore these things in detail in the coming chapters of the book.

Knowing this secret about the future means that understanding what's coming and shaping your future is possible. With a limited number of things to worry about, the future won't seem so overwhelming.

Before we dive in and get started, I want to give you one last tool to prepare you for the future. It's a bit of a defense mechanism. Because as you go about imagining, designing, and realizing your future, you're going to encounter people along the way who want you to believe some other version of the future. You don't have to listen and here's why.

Beware of Predictions and the People Who Make Them

Working as a futurist, people always expect me to make predictions about the future. It comes with the territory. This makes sense, but as I always respond, I'm not that kind of futurist. In fact, I'm a futurist who refuses to make predictions.

Why? Because predictions are useless. They're a fool's game.

One of my favorite quotes about predicting the future comes from Isaac Asimov, the sci-fi master known for his robot stories, which I absolutely love. But in his lifetime, Asimov was also known as the great explainer. He wrote far more books about science fact than he did about science fiction, across a range of disciplines, from astronomy to biology to chemistry to—well, I could probably make my way all the way down the alphabet, but you get the point. He even wrote about the Bible and world history.

But when it came to predicting the future, Asimov had a very specific stance. People always expected him, as a writer of science fiction and science fact, to predict the future. This led him to say:

> Predicting the future is a hopeless, thankless task, with ridicule to begin with and, all too often, scorn to end with.*

I always share this quote with my students on the first day of class. If you still want to be a futurist after hearing that, I say, then you've come to the right place.

As I also tell my students, futurists do not predict the future. It's not our job to *be right*. This is what most pundits and predictors of the future are trying to do. They want to be right. They want to be the person who gets up to stand in front of the camera and say "See? I told you so" when something they predicted comes to pass.

But this is not the job of a futurist—at least not my kind of applied futurism.

As an applied futurist, my job is not to be right but to *get it right*. That might seem like a subtle distinction, but it contains the whole universe of what I do. It basically means that when I'm working with clients, whether it's a small start-up or the government of Australia, I not only model possible and probable futures based on facts but also prepare the client so they're ready

---

*Isaac Asimov, "Life in 1990," *Diner's Club Magazine*, January 1965.

to achieve the best possible outcome. I help them design their future in such a way that they get it right and end up thriving.

This is what you and I are going to do together. I'm not going to tell you your future, but I am going to give you the tools and ways of thinking so you can get that future right and get the future you wanted.

There are a lot of people who like to make predictions about the future, people who enjoy telling you what your future is going to be like. Worse, there are people who want to scare you with overwhelming versions of the future that you can do nothing about. This is ridiculous. Anyone who tells you that a specific future is coming and there is nothing you can do about it is trying to disempower you.

Here's a simple way to combat the onslaught of negative futures and disempowering people you're likely to encounter as you begin to design your own future. Any time someone starts telling you about the future and making predictions, ask yourself these three questions:

- *Who are they?*

- *Why are they telling me this?*

- *What do they expect me to do with this information?*

Short and sweet, but I deliberately made these questions as simple and streamlined as possible so that when you're in front of the TV or on your laptop, maybe in the gym or the airport, and you hear a daunting prediction for the future, you can pause and quickly ask yourself them.

This Futurist at Your Front Door

This brings us to an important final point. You've invited me into your life to start talking about your future. (Okay, that feels like I'm a kind of futures vampire, but I'm going to ignore that for the moment.) I will not give you predictions. I will not tell you your future. I can give you different ways to think about the future, but it's only you who can know, and create, your future.

With that, I'm excited to show you how to think like a futurist so that you can begin the process of building your own future. The power begins when you start thinking like a futurist.

But first, here's a quick exercise to help get you in the right headspace.

PUTTING THE FUTURE TO WORK

Quick Questions 1

Time now for your first exercise.

This is the start of the Quick Questions that I talked about in chapter 1. Hopefully, you've found a journal that you'll use to complete this and other exercises through-out the book. As I explained, it really helps to have all your thoughts and ideas about the future in one place so that you can easily refer back to them. Futurecasting is a process. In that journey, your journal will become one of your most valu-able tools.

To begin the exercise, I just need you to answer the follow-ing questions. How long you spend on them depends on how you do your thinking, but I'd say longer than the time it takes to drink a cup of coffee, but don't go canceling your weekend plans or anything. Okay, here we go.

Part 1: Think About the Future

Fear of the unknown is the biggest fear of all for so many of us. Because the future feels like an enormous blind spot, it ex-ists as this big, scary, indescribable thing in our lives. And this makes for an ever-more-vicious cycle: the less you think you know about the future, the more you fear it, and as that fear builds, it blinds you even more to possible future outcomes. The purpose of the following exercise is to help you to break this cycle, to remove the fear and, with that, the blinders that keep you from imagining a new and better future for yourself and the closest people in your life.

QUESTION 1

What are your biggest fears about the future?

Let's kick things off with a simple brainstorm. I want you to tick off three or four future fears that keep you up at night. The fears might be related to job loss or the economy. Or maybe you're afraid of getting sick or that someone you love will fall ill. Or it could be the idea of growing old alone. Whichever fears come to mind first, jot them down and then move on to the next question.

FOLLOW-UP QUESTION:

- **Are there any small fears or worries that nag at you?**

What are the fears that hang around in your head during the day? These don't have to be big life-altering fears but the small stuff. Are you worried about getting out of shape? Are you spending too much time on technology?

QUESTION 2

What is the most recent prediction you've heard about the future?

As I talked about throughout this chapter, professional prognosticators are everywhere. Flip to the news and you'll quickly be bombarded. If not from the lips of a TV pundit, maybe the last prediction you heard came from the guy on the treadmill next to you at the gym, talking about this or that sure thing in the stock market. If you've heard more than one prediction recently, so much the better.

FOLLOW-UP QUESTIONS:

- **How did that prediction make you feel?**

- **What did it make you think about?**

Jot down a few words about how hearing these predictions made you feel. What did you see in your mind when you heard them? Did it change how you thought about the future? Was that a good thing or a bad thing? Why?

QUESTION 3

What is the furthest possible moment into the future that you can see?

The answer to this question will depend somewhat on your age. The younger you are, the further your future might extend, though you might still only be able to imagine life five or ten years out. Regardless, take a few minutes to imagine and describe the future that comes to mind. What kind of place are you in? Who are the people around you? What do you look like? Details are critical to futurecasting, so the more specific you can be here, the better.

FOLLOW-UP QUESTIONS:

- **What excites you about this far-off future?**

- **What worries you?**

This really is like trying a new workout routine: it requires muscles you probably aren't used to using. You might find it difficult. It might hurt, or at least annoy you a little, but it's worth it. Getting used to thinking about the future and articulating it is going to be a massively helpful tool for you to imagine, design, and reach your future.

Part 2: Talk About the Future

In this part of the exercise, I want you to pose these same questions to three other people in your life. Try for some diversity of age, gender, and background—maybe one friend, one relative, and one colleague. When you actively and intentionally seek answers from folks who may not share the same identity as you, you're looking for their innate answers, based on their personal experience. Someone who is from a different generation, someone whose skin color is different, someone who is a different gender, someone whose socio-economic status is different—you can bet that their perspectives and answers can open up things you may not have considered on your own.

When asking questions about the future, gaining these different points of view can bring new awareness and broaden your ideas.

Ask these people to write down their answers in an email or text, or take notes during a phone call or face-to-face. Either way, try to gather as many specific details as possible. If thinking about the future is going to be an important skill for you to get comfortable doing, then talking about the future is also essential. Remember, these are new exercises for the people you are talking to as well. They are not used to thinking about this. They might be uncomfortable. They might think it's silly. Bonus! This is a quick way for you to identify the unsupportive or toxic people in your life. These people could also become part of your team that helps you reach the future you are seeking.

Part 3: Reflect on the Future

In the final part of this exercise, I want you to compare and contrast your answers with those of your respondents. Now, I realize you're only a couple of chapters into the book, so I don't expect you to have completely altered your perception of the future. But hopefully some distinctions between your vision of the future and those of your respondents will be evident, given that you've started the process of redefining your relationship to the future.

Reflecting on the future is important because it gives you space and time to think. Most people don't give themselves time to just think about the future they want, to talk about it with other people and finally to reflect on it.

QUESTIONS:

- **What did you learn?**

- **Do you still want the same future?**

- **Did this change the future you now envision for yourself?**

Your future isn't fixed. It can change and you can change it. It's okay if your future changes as you begin to build it. That's a positive thing. Reflecting on your future gives you the space to get it right.

I'm in more or less a constant state of futurecasting with my life, so for me the differences are usually pronounced. Here are some of the patterns I've seen through years of doing this exercise.

- **A tendency toward doomsday.** I'm always struck by how quickly people land on the worst-case scenario when imagining the future. To use the example of death, I know it's inevitable, but it's not something I dwell on. Rather, my focus is on controlling the things in front of me. I eat well and exercise, get my annual checkups, and do everything I can to control the parts of my physical and mental health that I can control. This optimistic outlook is one of the best things my experience as a futurist has given me. Optimism or pessimism—being positive or negative about the future—is a choice. There is no right answer. It's up to you. Choosing to be positive about the future has great power. I want the same for you.

- **An inability to take predictions with a grain of salt.** Remember, predictions are a fool's game (and this from a futurist). My job is not to predict the future. It's to help people and organizations model various outcomes and determine the best possible one for them. As you begin to futurecast your life, that needs to be your primary objective as well. Don't try to predict the future. Do always prepare for it.

- **A dystopian vision of the future.** Blame Hollywood all you want, but we're all guilty of needing to be entertained by some seriously dark depictions of the future. I love sci-fi thrillers as much as the next person. But I also know that the vision being presented to me on-screen or in the pages of a novel is the creation of a paid entertainer. In real life, the future doesn't work that way. No matter how young or old you are, the world as you know it is not going to change all that much before your time here is up.

Okay, that concludes your first Quick Questions exercise. Give yourself a hand. No, really clap! Okay, if you won't clap then at least take a moment and feel good about it. Just like going to the gym or for a run, these exercises are work. They will not always be easy, but when you complete them, when you put in the effort, it's a big deal, and I would ask you to please take a moment and recognize that. Also remember to really thank the people who talked to you!

There will be more to come in subsequent chapters, including the next chapter, where we get down to the business of thinking like a futurist.

Up Next: Getting Down to Brass Tacks

Now that we've cleared away all the stubborn, long-held myths about the future, we can deal with its reality. Now you're ready to start thinking like a futurist. In chapter 3, I will pull back the curtain on the futurecasting process and walk you through my step-by-step methodology. Along the way, I'll share stories of various individuals who used the process to successfully identify and achieve the future they wanted.

How to Think Like a Futurist

S o you predict the future?" the woman asked skeptically.

"No, not at all, Mira," I replied, having spotted her name on the peel-and-stick badge on her lapel. "I work with people to explore their possible futures."

I was standing at the front of a boardroom in downtown Dallas, preparing to work with a large energy company, modeling not only the future of their business but also possible futures for the energy industry as a whole.

"For the next two days," I added, "we're going to look at both positive and negative futures and get your company pointed in the right direction."

"So what . . . you can see the future?" Mira asked, still not buying it. The rest of the room watched the exchange intently. I could tell that many of the execs on hand were thinking the same thing. Mira was the only one with enough courage to voice her skepticism.

"Not exactly," I said with a smile.

This might have been an antagonistic start to the workshop, but the truth is, I enjoy these kinds of discussions. I like to get people's true feelings and biases out in the open as quickly as possible. And when it comes to the power of futurism, there's no shortage of disbelievers. That's because, as I discussed at length in the previous chapter, everything most of us have been told about the future is wrong. When somebody like me gets up and offers an alternate vision of the future, there's a knee-jerk instinct to look askance. I'm okay with that.

"As a futurist, I have the tools and processes needed to help people like yourselves explore the future," I continued. "I'm not an expert in the future of energy, not by a long shot. You are. We're going to use my process and your expertise to explore the future of energy together."

Mira nodded and poured a glass of water from one of the glass pitchers sweating on the conference room table. I could tell she wanted to push back more, but she was being polite, not wanting to derail the discussion before it even got underway.

"I can't see the future, but I can show you how to change it," I added with a flourish.

"Wait, what?" she said, snapping back to attention, not expecting the sparring to continue.

"Say, can you just tell us who's going to win the Super Bowl?" a guy at the opposite end of the table interjected with a laugh. This was Frank, the manager who had brought me in for the workshop. "Now, that would be helpful!"

"I wish I could tell you that," I said, "but I don't want to disappoint any Cowboys fans in the room." More chuckles went around the table, and at that, people started to relax. Nothing like a little sports banter to put a boardroom at ease.

"Seriously, though," I continued, "I'm not in the business of predicting the future. But over the years, I've learned how to change it—not just explore possible and potential futures but actually alter its direction. The answer . . ." I allowed a dramatic pause here to focus the attention of the room.

"Well?" Mira asked.

"Please, BDJ, the suspense is killing us," Frank added, slapping the conference table with a little too much gusto.

"To change the future, you first need to change the story you're telling about it," I said. "If you can do that, if you can change the story you tell about your future self, you'll start to make different decisions, and those decisions will lead you to a whole new future. It's as simple as that. I've done it with companies like yours as well as governments and militaries. Change the story, change the future. It's the first critical step in futurecasting, and it's one we're all going to take together, starting right now."

I looked over at Mira to see if my toughest skeptic showed any signs of warming. Like any top executive, she had a pretty good poker face. But after a beat or two, there was a barely perceptible nod of the head and raising of the eyebrows. It was all the opening I needed.

The 1-2-3 of Futurecasting

Over the course of the next two days in Dallas, I shared with Mira and company the futurecasting process I've developed and honed over the last three decades. In this chapter, I'm going to share the process with you.

As I told the team in Dallas, the first and most important step is to change the story you tell yourself about the future you want to live in. To do that you need to imagine yourself in a different future. You need to come up with a new story of your future. As I'll discuss in greater detail later, there are many different strategies for arriving at this new narrative. For now, just understand that you can't change the future until you grab hold of the narrative.

After you create your story, the second step in the process is to identify the forces that will get you to your new future. These "future forces" include the supportive *people* who can help you, the *tools* that will propel you through your new story, and the *experts* who have been there before. I'll show you how to identify and tap into these three resources to keep your new future on track.

Once you see yourself in a different future and identify your future forces, the third and final step is to do what I call "backcasting." It involves determining the specific steps you need to take to move toward the future you want and to avoid the future you don't want. This can feel daunting, but by breaking the process down into incremental steps, it will feel more doable. I call this part of the process backcasting because you work backward to determine these steps: you will first imagine what you need to do to get *halfway* to your different future, then what you need to do to move even *partway* toward that future, then what you need to do right away, or *Monday*, as I call it.

Futurecasting is all about movement. Being able to get started and then build and maintain momentum is critical to the entire process. I can't tell you how many futures haven't been realized because people simply don't know where to begin. They overthink the situation and end up in a state of analysis paralysis. If imagination is the first rule of futurecasting, action is a close second.

So that's the process in a nutshell. In the following sections of this chapter, I've included more details, as well as examples, exercises, and strategies. Then you'll read about a woman who used the process to find a new career she really wanted. You'll also meet other people I've worked with who have futurecasted different aspects of their lives—everything from love and relationships to money and finance to health and wellness. I'll end the chapter with another exercise for you to begin to try out some futurecasting for yourself.

I tell my students all the time, "The process is the process."

Whatever future you're looking to create, by applying this process, anything is possible.

Holding Futurists Accountable

I have taught futurists for over a decade. I can say with great pride that my students have gone on to be futurists at some of the world's largest corporations, governments, and nonprofits.

For the past eight years, my students have been required to read one book before the first day of class: *Future Babble* by Dan Gardner. Dan is a consultant, a *New York Times* bestselling author of books about psychology and decision-making, and a senior fellow at the University of Ottawa's Graduate School of Public and International Affairs.

In *Future Babble*, Dan applies the diligence of an investigative journalist in shining a harsh light on futurists and futurism, showing with painstaking detail how the predictions that futurists have made over the years have been incredibly wrong. As part of my research for this book, I decided to reach out to Dan to see how he would frame futurecasting for people who are coming at the process for the first time.

"When I was writing *Future Babble* back in 2009, people were really concerned with the price of oil," Dan explained to me, by way of an example, in a recent early morning phone call. "Everyone wanted to know if we had hit 'peak oil.' Had oil prices reached their limit?"

"I remember well," I told him.

"Since then, the events that have happened around the price of oil were predicted by nobody." Dan chuckled. "If you had predicted where we are today back in 2009, people would have thought you were crazy. It just goes to show how even the so-called experts get it wrong time and again. Even when we try to be broad-minded, our thinking is usually too narrow."

"So what advice would you give regular people who are trying to imagine and build their own future?" I asked, getting right down to the point.

"Balance," Dan began. "People need to strike a balance between two different desires or ideas. The first is our inherent desire for certainty. We want to know exactly what will happen in the future. So we look to experts who we think can tell us for sure what we can expect."

"That's why people accept predictions when they really shouldn't," I added.

"Yes," Dan said. "The second idea we need to balance is

that the future is uncertain and anything could happen. Neither of these ideas will be one hundred percent true. The trick is to balance them."

"What advice would you give people to strike this balance?" I asked.

"Humility," Dan answered firmly. "The certainty business is a big mistake. But people who are humble have a far better chance of success. They're the ones who, when asked what will happen five years in the future, will start by telling you that they don't know exactly. But then they will tell you their thought process and what they would do to try and answer the question."

"That's what I tell my students all the time," I said. "It's not about being right. It's about getting it right."

"As we walk toward our future, we can't be scared and keep our heads down," Dan said, wrapping up the conversation. "We can't keep staring at our feet out of fear of the unknown. People need to keep their heads up and keep their eyes on the future with a plan for how to think about what's over the horizon."

A Deep Dive into the Futurecasting Process

Step 1: The Future You—
Creating the Story of Your Future

Nothing great ever built by humans wasn't imagined first. The first step in the process is to ask yourself this one basic question: *What is the future I want?* I know that sounds incredibly simple, but for so many of my clients, it's the hardest hurdle to leap. They just don't know what kind of future they want. And the reason they don't is that they've never given themselves permission to ponder the question in the first place, for all the reasons enumerated in the previous chapter—they think the future is fixed, they think it's inevitable, they're too scared to even contemplate it, etc.

Even when people feel like they have permission to imagine the future, they tend to lack any kind of platform for turning this imagined future into a reality. Futurecasting provides both the permission and the platform.

So, Step 1 . . . what is the future you want? As you consider this question, it's important to be as detailed and specific as possible.

I once worked with a guy called Tim who, at the ripe old age of forty, found himself in the worst physical shape of his life. Other aspects of his life were good—happy marriage, nice kids, a stable job—but his deteriorating physical health was a major drag on his happiness.

"What's the future you want?" I asked him in our first meeting.

"I want to feel good," Tim answered. "I want to lead a more healthy life."

"Okay, what does that look like exactly?" I asked.

"I'm not sure," he said.

I told him he needed to figure that out, and I asked a bunch of leading questions. I'm not a personal trainer or an expert in nutrition, but I didn't have to be one to get Tim thinking about his future health in very specific terms. The next time we met, he presented his plan.

"Okay, BDJ, here we go. I'm 225 pounds today. I want to get down to 190, the weight I was when I played lacrosse in college. My cholesterol is 256. Target there is 195. Triglycerides are 217. I need them to be 150 or lower. As I stand here today, I can't walk up a flight of stairs without losing my breath. My goal is to run a 5K in twenty-five minutes within three months."

There was more to Tim's action plan, but you get the picture. To start in on your future, you need to be specific. As I noted in chapter 1, it's important to write down the details, preferably with a pen and paper, or at least type the words out. The physical action of writing will help get you thinking, and seeing your goals and objectives is a big step toward making them a reality.

If you get stuck and find yourself staring at a blank sheet of paper, think about coming at the problem from another direction, by asking yourself about the future you want to avoid. I use this tactic a lot with companies and corporations, whose leaders are often worried about negative outcomes from macro-forces like cyberattacks or a sudden currency collapse. They don't want their business to be adversely affected by these macro-forces. I refer to this as "threatcasting," a subset of futurecasting, and it can be easily applied to individual lives as well.

Maybe you want to avoid a future in which you don't have enough money to maintain your current standard of living. Or you're worried that your marriage is going to fall apart. (Hey, a good many of them do, right? And often over issues that might have been avoided with a little more forward thinking.) By considering the future you want to avoid, you will be able to reverse engineer the future you want. Whichever tack you take, the important thing is to be as specific as possible. Remember, you're telling yourself the new story of your future, and any good story has to include plenty of detail.

One final word on the storytelling piece of the process: the future is powerful. I take my job very seriously. Over the decades, I've had a front-row seat to tomorrow. I've seen people—from massive organizations to regular folks—change their futures. I've seen it happen, and every time it's humbling. Anyone can change their future. You can change your future.

This kind of thinking is empowering and it will change your life. We all know that dreams are magic. They can inspire us or, in the case of nightmares, strike terror in our hearts. Dreams get inside us and touch us in ways average stories might not.

This is my challenge to you: dare to dream a different dream—a dream of a future that you really and truly want. Because it is possible. If you can dream a bold new dream and truly believe in it . . . you will change your future.

Step 2: Future Forces—Propelling Yourself Toward Your Future

The future doesn't just happen. I will continue to hammer that home throughout the course of the book. The future is shaped by forces that propel your life in positive or negative directions. Once you've created the story of the new future you want for yourself, you need to figure out the specific forces that you will rely on to get you there.

As previously mentioned, these forces fall into three categories: people, tools, and experts. Taking the time to explore and identify each of these three is key. I'm not going to sugarcoat it. This leg of the futurecasting journey takes a lot of work. It's labor-intensive and time-consuming. When I'm working with a major client, like a Fortune 500 company or a division of the military, I'll allow three to six months for "future-forcing."

You might not need to go to that extreme, but this is not the kind of project you can knock out in a weekend. It requires thorough research and deep, meditative thinking. What's more, it's not the sort of thinking you've done much of before, so your brain will need time to fire up different synapses, the same way your muscles need time to adapt to a new workout routine. Everyone is different, but my advice to clients is to allow at least two weeks for the initial future-forcing process. Plus, recognize that this will always be a work in progress. You'll need to revisit your plan from time to time as you start moving toward the future you want.

Also, understand that this step in the process is going to make you feel uncomfortable. Anything meaningful, especially having to do with your future, should make you feel a little uneasy at times. That sinking feeling, that drop in your stomach, maybe even that nervous sweat you break into at odd moments—these are all indicators that you're doing the right thing.

This is what real change feels like. I tell my clients that of course this is hard and uncomfortable. That's why we call it real-life work. That's why it matters and gets results. If it was effortless, we would call it watching TV.

Okay, let's get started.

People: Building Your Team

People are the most important force in anyone's life. People build the future. But they don't build it alone. As you put together your action plan for moving toward the future you've envisioned, you will need the support of a community. You will need your people. You will need your team.

These are the individuals in your life you can count on to support you through this journey. Start with people you trust implicitly and who care about your future the most. Family and friends are the obvious candidates, though coworkers can also be good sources. There's no magic number here, but I recommend a support team of no fewer than five people, at least in the beginning.

Once you figure out the circle, you need to meet with them individually and share your story. Make the meeting official—lunch on Tuesday at 1 p.m., a coffee before work on Thursday, a beer after this weekend's game, etc. I don't want you try to share your story while you're walking down the hall at work in between meetings. The future is precious. It needs to be handled so.

You can share the story in written form ahead of time or tell it in person. Either way, it's probably going to have you feeling vulnerable and exposed. That's a good thing! Being truly vulnerable is the quickest path to building trust with another person.

The reason you're sharing your story is twofold. First, it creates a measure of accountability. Sharing your story makes it real, and it also means you're officially on watch. I've even had clients who, after sharing their story with an inner circle of friends, went hyper-public by posting it on social media. I'm a little ambivalent about the impact of social media on society, but this is one instance in which it offers real value.

In addition to creating accountability, sharing your story with your team is a way to get feedback. Keep this in mind when you're pulling together your list of people for the team. You need individuals who won't be afraid to speak their mind and give it to you straight. Some of them might think your plan is wonderful, while others might try to poke holes.

The story of the future you is powerful because it not only will allow you to bring that future into being but also can identify toxic people in your life. If you encounter someone who doesn't believe in your future, for reasons that don't necessarily have anything to do with you or your project, you might start to realize that this relationship isn't very healthy.

Bottom line: be open and listen closely throughout the process. Any feedback, bad or good, will help refine your vision. Every conversation you have with your team will solidify, expand, and ultimately bring into focus your future. And the people you share your future with will be your allies along the way. Remember, life is a team sport.

So how do you find them? If your future will only be as bright as the team you assemble to build it, where and how do you go looking? While there's no one simple answer to that question, through my years of futurecasting, I've developed several strategies that work for me.

For starters, *always practice reciprocity.* These relationships don't have to be transactional per se. Remember, most people enjoy helping others, so it shouldn't be based on a quid pro quo. However, it's always a good idea to figure out ways that you might be useful to the people who are helping you out. They might not have any needs at the moment, but making it clear to them that you're available should any needs arise will leave the relationship on very solid ground.

Next, *always strive to be a connector*. As your team grows, there will start to be more and more crossover. Get in the habit of connecting the dots when you identify people who will benefit from knowing one another. You're only as strong as your overall network, and being a constant connector is a great way to improve your network's health and vitality.

This next piece of advice should be obvious: *avoid toxic relationships*. So many people have a hard time doing this, to the enormous detriment of their future. While I generally preach the virtue of inclusion, some people just aren't *your* people. Toxicity is the biggest red flag of all. It takes different forms. The most common example is the person who doesn't support your vision of the future. Maybe they're jealous of your ambition, or maybe they don't have enough creative vision to see the possibilities of what you're trying to do. Whatever the reason for their toxicity, it's a threat to your success, so you need to kick them off the team, and probably out of your life as well.

Another important rule: *keep it real*. Authenticity is one of the most important qualities in futurecasting. It starts with being true to yourself, by allowing yourself to dream the big dream. Then you need to be genuine with the people you meet. I give this advice frequently to shy, reserved types, who often freak out at the very notion of networking. If you're an introvert, don't think you have to fake being an extrovert at networking events. Own your shyness and humility. It will endear you to the right people for you.

Last but not least: *always be networking.* Futurecasting isn't a one-and-done practice. I truly think of it as a way of life. As a result, it pays to be on the lookout at all times for potential team members who add value to you. I can't tell you how many times I've been at a conference or dinner party and I've met someone whose insights and perspective I appreciate. I always make a point of trading contact info and following up with a quick note in the next few days. With that follow-up, the person goes from being a casual acquaintance to a member of my team, and I'll have no problem calling on their expertise at some point in the future.

You have already started doing this. Your Quick Questions exercise from chapter 2 works as a great first pass at identifying your people and finding your team, getting comfortable in your own mind and thinking about your future. Being able to talk about the future with people who are supportive and open-minded is key. You can tell them about the future you and then listen to them when they tell you about their future. There is magic in that exchange. You will affect each other's future in positive ways. If you don't feel energized and supported after a conversation with a person, take a step back and reflect on whether to include that person in your team.

Quick Reflection: The Power of Uncomfortable Conversations

Whenever you reflect on an uncomfortable conversation you had with someone, ask yourself these questions:

- *Why did the conversation get uncomfortable?*

- *Was the person negative or dismissive? Did they disagree with a core part of your idea? Of you? Was their disagreement unexpected?*

- *Were they challenging? Did I learn anything?*

The conversations you have with people, with your team, need to be positive. They also should be challenging and uncomfortable at times. There is an important difference between being dismissed and being challenged. When a person dismisses you, they don't recognize your worth and humanity. This is terrible. Get away from that person. But when a person challenges you with positive intent, possibly pushing you to see the world in a different way, that is a gift.

Humans don't like feeling uncomfortable. You probably

saw that while doing the exercise in chapter 2. Try to get comfortable with feeling uncomfortable. You don't have to agree with the person but if you really want to get the most out of the conversation, it's important to get curious. First, acknowledge out loud that what they just said made you uncomfortable and explain the reasons. Next, tell them you value what they said but could they re-explain or re-phrase it.

These kinds of conversations are how we change and grow and learn. Uncomfortable conversations can shape your vision of the future you, even make that vision more grounded and achievable. Making sure that you find the right people for your team, people you can have uncomfortable conversations with, will make the future you a reality.

Once your team is in place, think about the best way to engage them. Some people will be willing and able to talk, while others might not know how to react or respond. I run into this all the time, even within companies and corporations that are paying good money for my consultation. Responses range from defensive to nervous to downright defiant. I never take it personally, and neither should you (even though you'll be talking on a much more personal level). If you really value a person's opinion but think they might have trouble delivering, it's particularly important to come up with a ready list of questions. You might ask them, "Does the future I'm describing make sense to you?" Or "Have I given you enough detail?" And one of my favorites, "If you were me, what are the first steps you would take toward achieving this future?" Getting your team member to imagine themselves in your shoes will help them engage in the process and also take the pressure off them to have all the answers. A good direct question to ask at the end of a conversation is "Do you think this will work?" You are giving that person the chance to air any doubts they may be holding back.

Tools: Gathering Resources to Propel You

Assembling your team and getting their feedback is important to the task of building your future. But there are forces beyond people. That takes us to tools. These are not people but material resources. These enabling forces will help you create your new future and sustain it over time

Tools are drawn from various categories. That's because everyone's future is different and so the enabling forces will be different depending on the future that's being built. Tools also take many forms. They often exist online, in the form of digital products and services designed to reach a goal, whether it's to help you find a new job, make a love connection, or get your financial house in order. Another tool might be an organization, such as an industry trade group that can facilitate networking. For someone looking to change their social life, tools might take the shape of a community center or a local religious institution.

As you start to identify your tools, don't worry if the list feels too long and scattered at first. You'll continue to refine and define as you move through the process. For example, let's say you want to make a career change. Maybe the story of the future you created for yourself involves a move from finance into education. You've gotten constructive feedback from friends and family. Now you need a more specific direction. Your list of tools might include a book or two on the current state of education, a networking group of educators in your area, and financial software that can help you navigate the potential reduction in income.

I should add that this phase of the process, which again should take at least two weeks, doesn't always move in a straight line. Over the course of the process, your tools may morph as you grow personally and your future begins to take shape. Oftentimes people will tack from one resource to another, like the back-and-forth movement of a sailboat. But as with sailing, they're always moving forward despite the sideways motion, using each new enabling tool to propel them in the right direction.

In fact, being comfortable with moving from one resource to the next is part of the power of future-forcing. It embraces the idea that no meaningful process in life follows a straight line. Journeys are fluid. We move from place to place, person to person, resource to resource. Each step of the way teaches us something new about the process, and reveals the next move we need to make.

Though tools vary depending on the future that's being created, a few general best practices apply for pulling them together. For starters, it's important to tailor the tool to the task. If you aim to build a brick wall, you'll need a trowel; for a spindle-backed chair, you'll lean on the lathe. It's the same with futurecasting. Career seekers can choose from an array of websites and online tools, like LinkedIn and Glassdoor. Dating apps abound for those looking for love, from Bumble to Tinder to Match. People intent on finding the perfect place to live can take advantage of tools like NeighborhoodScout, Redfin, and Zillow. If you prefer to do your research offline, look to your local library for a trove of helpful books and articles.

It's also important to think about what's right for you. Strategic tools and resources run the gamut from data driven and analytical to emotion based. There's no one-size-fits-all. Think about how you like to work and which goal-driven strategies you've been successful with in the past. Some people thrive on data and analytics, in which case software-based tools might be the best fit. For those who thrive on feelings and emotions, journal-based tools will probably be the way to go. Know yourself, know your tools, know your future.

I tend to focus on technology when talking about resources, but it's important to remember that people are still valuable in this phase of future-forcing. Often they're the best sources of referrals, suggesting websites to check out or organizations to contact. Futurecasting always involves a bit of detective work. If you're running into a bunch of dead ends in your search for tools, don't hesitate to pick up the phone or tap out an email to get insights from another human being.

Finally, remember the rule of give-and-take. I talked about the importance of reciprocity when building out your team. The same lesson applies with tools. If you identify an organization that you think might be helpful to your futurecasting, research ways you can support them, ideally before reaching out to them. For example, if you're looking to join a networking organization, find out if they're looking for people to volunteer at upcoming events, and offer up your services during the initial meeting or call. It will endear you to the folks in charge and open doors more quickly.

Experts: Seeking Out the People Who Have Been There Before

At this stage in the future-forcing process, the story of your future will be in sharp focus and you should have the beginnings of an action plan. The final force for you to explore is the experts. These are the people who will give you the exact direction and information you need to realize your future.

The whole notion of expertise has come under some assault in recent years, along with things like science and fact-based information. I won't wade too far into that politically charged debate, but I will submit that expertise matters hugely in the context of futurecasting because it requires such depth of experience. There's a great book originally published in 1999 that I still encourage my students to read called *How People Learn: Brain, Mind, Experience, and School.* In one favorite passage, the authors write, "Experts notice features and meaningful patterns of information that are not noticed by novices."* This pattern spotting is so valuable to futurecasting, and it's why experts are the final, and in many ways the most powerful, force in the whole process.

Start by looking for people who have made a similar journey. Back to the example of Tim, my out-of-shape fortysomething client: his first action was to look for people who had managed to get back into shape in middle age. After a bit of asking around, he tracked down an old teammate from college who had been through a similar health journey, with positive results in the end. Over the course of several conversations, Tim was able to expand the list of experts he would need to fulfill his mission: a personal trainer to establish a fitness plan, a nutritionist to help with diet, a yoga and meditation instructor to provide spiritual balance, and so on. Everyone's future is individual. Your future is unlike Tim's, or any other person's, for the simple reason that your life is your own. Likewise, your list of experts will be unique.

Once you have your list of experts, the next step is to enlist their help and learn everything you can from them. This is the

---

*National Research Council, *How People Learn: Brain, Mind, Experience, and School*, eds. John D. Bransford, Ann L. Brown, and Rodney R. Cocking (Washington, DC: National Academy Press, 2000), 31.

sponge stage in the process, even more so than with your team of people. You need to absorb every detail you can. If the expert is someone whose future you want to emulate, understand everything you can about what they did to get to where they are. Even if their future isn't exactly in line with your own aspirations, as long as their connection, their journey, their insights, and their network of people will be helpful to you.

As with most aspects of futurecasting, the process can be uncomfortable, especially if your list of experts includes strangers. As I've said already, the work is hard and it's meant to get you pushing yourself beyond your comfort zone. This isn't watching TV. This is realizing your future.

When you begin the process of talking with experts, you'll discover something amazing: people like to help other people. Experts like to share the knowledge they've attained through their life's work. It's important that you respect their time and come to the meeting prepared. But if you do that, I think you'll be surprised by how giving people can be. Any successful person will know that enabling the success of others by connecting passionate, like-minded people benefits everyone involved. These experts will be your mentors, your collaborators, and in some cases even your new friends.

So where do you find experts? Well, they're people too, so many of the rules for building your team apply here as well, including around networking and reciprocity. But in most cases, the experts you'll want to engage with will be strangers, often high-powered ones. That means you'll need to be a bit more deliberate in your approach.

Good preparation should precede any new meetings in life, but it's absolutely essential when you're approaching someone whose expertise you value and wish to benefit from. Knowing key details about their background (where they grew up, where they went to school, how long they've been in their current role) will facilitate the conversation through the early stages and show your expert that you're genuinely interested in them. Plus, let's face it: flattery goes a long way, but especially with people in positions of power.

Part of the prep work involves putting together a list of questions. In the spirit of flattery, don't be shy about asking them about their life and journey. "What is the path you took to get to where you are today?" "What were the most important steps you took to get you there?" "Who are the most important people who helped along the way?" And be sure to take advantage of their network and experience by seeing if there are any other experts they think you should contact.

It's also important to listen closely. This should be obvious, but in our nervousness, we often end up overtalking, when the smart thing is to shut up and listen. As part of your preparation, come up with a concise summary of why you wanted to meet them and what you're hoping to learn, then give your expert plenty of time to talk. Have a few follow-up questions at the ready in case they're not as forthcoming as you'd hoped. Not all experts are extroverts, so you might have to work hard for the information.

Once you get in the room, try to stay relaxed and confident. Yes, you should respect your expert's time and defer to their knowledge and expertise. But that doesn't mean you have to shortchange your ambitions. Remember what I said about the importance of being bold when coming up with the story of your future. That same confidence needs to come through in your expert meeting. Provided it's coming from a genuine place, I doubt that anyone would ever try to belittle your ambition. And if for some reason they did, you would know very quickly that this one expert is definitely not for you.

Step 3: Begin Backcasting

Now that you have a clear vision for your future and understand the forces that will help propel you there, it's time to figure out the precise steps you'll need to take to get there. It's time to backcast.

I always love this moment in the process when I'm working with a client. After weeks of research and interviews and intense questioning, culminating in the modeling of futures good and bad, the moment comes to get down to brass tacks and apply what we've learned to the creation of a concrete action plan. That's what being an *applied* futurist is all about.

For the average person, the process can seem incredibly daunting. It's easy to feel like there's a massive expanse between where you are today and the future you've imagined for yourself. Trust me when I say, it's closer than you think.

Backcasting is the secret to closing the gap, by identifying the specific steps you need to take to reach your goals. Once again, details are critical, as they're what will turn your future from abstract to actionable. By focusing on the details, the massive expanse will not feel so massive.

To get started, I want you to divide your actions into three phases:

- halfway,

- partway, and

- Monday.

Here's a sketch I drew up some years ago to help a client visualize the process, including the backcast as well as the earlier future forces of the program:

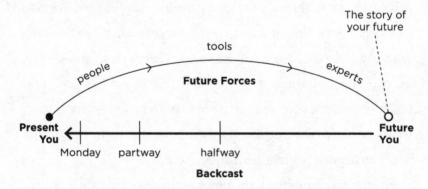

I now give it to everyone I work with, including you. Hopefully it will help to convince you that a seemingly Herculean effort of changing the future is actually quite simple and streamlined.

With that, let's go into a little more detail with regards to how the backcast works.

Determining the Halfway Point

To begin this process, I want you to ask yourself what needs to happen to get you halfway between where you are today and where you ultimately want to be. Let's use the example of a career change, since it's one I confront so often. The fully realized future in this scenario might involve you comfortably settled in a new job. Let's pretend the process took eighteen months, start to finish. What did the halfway point look like? Nine months in, maybe you were finally ready to give notice to your current employer. Or maybe you were ready to enroll in the coursework needed to make the career transition possible.

Because halfway is, well, halfway, it's okay if the details are still somewhat uncertain. The future is still fairly far out. The goal is to be as specific as possible, knowing that you'll return to the action plan as the journey gets underway to fill in more details as you learn.

Next Stop: Partway

With an idea of what getting 50 percent of the way to your future will look like, the next step in the process is to get a quarter of the way there. This goal should be a little bit easier to see. For the career changer, it might involve identifying and applying to three continuing education programs that you will need to qualify for a job in your new chosen field.

Finding the partway point is exciting because it's often the first concrete step you take toward moving in a different direction. It's that moment when you've officially left your undesirable present behind and started the work of moving toward that future you want.

And Finally . . . Monday

That takes us to Monday, or the actions you can take right away. It's the easiest part of the process since you're usually not talking about heavy-lift action items. Maybe it's opening a separate savings account at your bank where you'll put away money for future coursework or for the period of time when you'll be without a steady paycheck. Monday can also refer back to the future-forcing process—for example, refining your future story or tweaking the list of people you will share the story with once it's finished.

Whatever Monday looks like to you, the important thing is to get started by taking clear and specific actions. Once you're off the starting block, you'll see that the future you've imagined is closer, and more attainable, than you ever dared to imagine.

The Secret of Futurecasting: It's All About the Process

Futurecasting helps people to envision the future they want, to identify the forces that will propel them forward, and to figure out the specific steps to take to get there. In short, it's a process.

But it's not a process you complete quickly. I like to tell my clients that if they can imagine, design, and build their future in a day, they're doing it all wrong. The future takes work.

As you go through the process, you'll continue to look back on what you've accomplished. You'll reread the story of your future to make sure it's still accurate and on track. Maybe what you've learned needs to be altered, refined, or given more detail. Things might happen in your life or you might be introduced to a new concept that inspires you to adapt your story. That's okay. The future you is always in motion. It will change as you change. The process allows individuals to continue to explore the future they want and not be locked into a single future. The simple truth is that the future is the motion, the work, and the journey that will get you to where you want to be, time and time again.

Now that you know the process, I want you to meet Susan. She's a person I worked with who was looking to make a change but wasn't sure what she wanted. Like so many of us, Susan knew only that she no longer wanted to do what she was doing. Her present was unacceptable, but her future was unclear. Working together, we used futurecasting to figure out what she wanted to be when she grew up—and how to go out and get it.

A quick note before we jump in: Though I'm not a doctor, I afford everyone I talk with a doctor-patient privilege similar to that of a trained therapist or physician. Out of respect for people's privacy and their trust in me, I've changed the names, and some telling biographical details, of all the individuals included in this book. However, every person you're about to meet, starting with Susan from Chicago, is based on someone real with an actual future that needed to be recast.

Learning What You Want to Be
When You Grow Up

A cold wind cut through the streets of Chicago as I hustled to my morning appointment. It was the first really cold day of winter and I was underdressed—not something to be proud of if you're a person who gets paid to envision the future. But apart from the stiff breeze blowing in off Lake Michigan, it was a beautiful, sunny day in the windy city.

As I walked into the coffee shop, the bustle of the street gave way to a warm, relaxing hum. The shop was filled with the kinds of people you would expect to find at 10:30 a.m. on a Wednesday. Students with big headphones tapping away at laptops. Tourists huddled around tables, taking in the retro bohemian vibe, planning for a day of sightseeing. And a handful of professionals quietly taking calls or answering emails on their phones.

I was in town to meet with one of my private-practice clients, Susan, a fortysomething marketing executive at a major technology company.

We'd met a few years back at a conference, done some work together here and there, but mostly stayed in touch through our social networks. It had been about six months since our last direct contact, so I wasn't sure what to expect when she reached out and asked to meet for coffee.

I didn't see Susan anywhere in the shop, so I grabbed a black coffee from the barista and snagged one of the last empty tables. A few minutes later, Susan stormed through the door, made a beeline for me, dumped her bags, gave me a quick hug, and ran off to get a green tea.

Susan's whirlwind exterior gave the impression of dishevelment, but I knew better. This was a highly successful executive, well respected in her company, throughout the industry, and indeed around the world. Still, I could tell something was amiss.

When she returned to the table, I smiled and asked, "How can I help?"

"I don't know what I want to be when I grow up," Susan replied with a short, uncomfortable laugh. "Really, BDJ, I've been thinking about it, and I really don't know what I want to be when I grow up." She gave a deep sigh, swirling her tea with a wooden stirrer.

I've been here many times before, with many other clients. It's the moment when they're first trying to imagine their future and all they can see is a huge yawning chasm of nothingness. It's terrifying for them. For me, it's kind of thrilling. It means the chase is on.

"I know I don't want to keep doing the same job I have now," Susan went on, snapping back into the present moment. "Don't get me wrong, I like the work and the people, but I never thought I'd be forty-six years old and doing this . . ."

"That makes sense," I answered. "So how can I help?"

"What do you think I should do?"

Career advice. It's easily the most frequent topic of conversation I have with people. They want to know what they should do with their lives. Or what their kids should do with their lives. Or, as was the case with Susan, how to pivot midcareer to the job they had always wanted, instead of the one they had somehow ended up in.

These are all tricky questions because, at their core, they're not about work or career planning. They're instead precursors to the question most people find the hardest to answer: What makes you happy?

Happiness is a hard one. In fact, it's so elusive that there are entire college courses and research programs devoted to its study. Several years ago, I went to one of the leading experts in the field to get guidance on how to help people like Susan figure out what makes them happy.

Scott Cloutier is an assistant professor and a senior sustainability scientist at the Julie Ann Wrigley Global Institute of Sustainability at Arizona State University. He is focused on charting a new course for sustainability to maximize opportunities for happiness. I had caught up with him in Tempe, Arizona, one lovely winter's day in the desert and asked him about happiness.

"Happiness is a spectrum," he started, leaning back in his chair. "On the one end you have sadness, and the other end is all-out bliss. Happiness is about finding balance on the spectrum."

"So when people are trying to decide what to do with their lives . . ." I said, trailing off. Then, more specifically: "When they are trying to see themselves in a future career, how should they think about what will help them find that perfect balance?"

"There are two things to consider," Scott said, holding up two fingers. "Pleasure and purpose. You need to know the difference. Pleasure is easy. Right now we could walk down the street and get whatever pleasure we want. Food, sex, alcohol, drugs—you name it. Our world is filled with pleasure. The problem is, it's immediate and empty. It will not make you happy."

"If pleasure isn't the key," I said, "can I assume purpose is the key?"

"You can indeed," Scott answered. "Purpose is the thing that gets you going. It's the thing that gives you meaning. It allows you to have a vision of the person you want to become so you can hold that vision in your mind as you dance through the complexities of life."

I thought about how many people I'd met over the years who, at least on the face of it, seemed to have it all—beautiful family, big house, money in the bank. The only thing missing was a true sense of contentment. As I scanned through these people in my mind, I realized they did all struggle with a lack of purpose.

"So if people can just identify a purpose, their path to happiness will become clear?" I asked.

"Yes, it will." Scott smiled. "There's nothing wrong with a pleasure-filled life, but it won't make you happy in the long run."

With that conversation in mind, I asked Susan a few questions to get her thinking about her purpose. I needed her to imagine herself in a future that would make her happy. I needed her to imagine where she wanted to spend her time over the next couple of decades.

We talked for a while, bouncing from subject to subject, but it was obvious that Susan was struggling to find clarity, so finally I asked a question I thought she'd be able to answer: "Do you want to be rich?"

"What's that?" she said. The question had clearly taken her by surprise. "I mean, who doesn't want to be rich? Doesn't everybody want to be rich?"

"Sure, everybody wants to be rich," I answered. "But few people know what kind of rich they want to be."

"What does that mean?" Susan asked with a sideways glance.

"Let's try this," I said, taking another sip of coffee. "Do you want to be yacht rich?"

"Yacht rich? I'm still not sure I understand what you mean."

"Do you want to be so rich that you own a yacht? It's a pretty simple question."

Susan thought for a moment and then shook her head and replied, "No, I don't want a yacht. I don't even know where I'd store a yacht."

"Okay, great. That's a start. Do you want to be mansion rich?"

"Like, do you mean do I want to own a mansion?" she asked.

"Exactly. Do you want to be so rich that you can have a massive mansion with a pool, tennis court, five-car garage, and enough staff to care for it all? Do you want to be mansion rich?"

"Honestly, that doesn't sound bad, but it might freak out my husband, Patrick."

I paused here to explain that defining the future requires incredible attention to detail. To illustrate the point, I told her about the time I helped a global supply chain trade association plan for the digital future. The group's leaders knew that technologies like autonomous vehicles, big data, and artificial intelligence were going to disrupt traditional supply chains in seismic ways. But they didn't know the specific steps they needed to take right away to prepare for these fundamental changes. After futurecasting possibilities, I helped them identify new job roles that had to be created as well as the retraining of their current workforce that had to happen to minimize forced staff reductions and increase transparency and sustainability throughout the industry.

"The same attention to detail is needed when figuring out what kind of lifestyle you envision for yourself," I told Susan. "It's not enough to say you want to be rich. You need to know what kind of rich you want to be. Is it mansion rich or is it mortgage-paid-off, college-fund-secure, enough-savings-to-retire rich?"

Susan and I went on talking for a while, discussing her future in more detail. She didn't want to be a marketing executive anymore. She didn't want to work at a large corporation. Unfortunately, figuring out what she did want to do—that is, figuring out her purpose—was proving more elusive, and it's not the kind of problem that can be solved over a cup of tea. The important thing, though, was that the futurecasting process was underway. Getting started is always the biggest hurdle.

"What do you say?" I asked. "Should we pick this up next time?"

"Okay," she answered. "Just don't forget your crystal ball." For the first time all morning, her brow softened and there was even the hint of a smile in her eyes. The future wasn't clear yet, but I could sense her relief that she was starting to bring it into focus.

While my conversation with Susan that morning was somewhat meandering, my intention was very targeted: to bring her to the first, critical step in futurecasting, creating the story of her future. Susan didn't know what she wanted, but she knew she wanted a change. My questions were meant to force her to consider her future in more detail. "Not doing what I'm doing today" is not nearly specific enough when it comes to building the future. Sometimes it helps to explore the effects of the change you want to make. That's why I asked Susan if she wanted to be "yacht rich." I love asking people this question because it catches them off guard, and that's the moment when people more easily get specific and really interrogate themselves about the future they want.

Six Months Later

I was back in Chicago. Spring was in full bloom, with a hint of humidity in the air. On my swing through town, I carved out time to check in with Susan. She'd been keeping me in the loop on her futurecasting progress via Skype and email, but I wanted to get the full report in person.

This time we met at a small pizza joint in the burbs. It was 2:30 p.m., and the place was quiet. The lunch rush had emptied out, and happy hour folks had yet to arrive.

"Well," I said, "how are things going?

"I quit my job," Susan said, beaming with happiness.

"Oh?" I said. I hadn't heard that part in any of our recent exchanges.

"Yeah, I did it two days ago. It's not public knowledge, but I thought you should know because it's all to do with you."

"Well, I don't know about that," I protested.

"No, really," she said, leaning forward. "I took your advice and sat down with my husband and we talked through the possible futures we wanted for ourselves. It's funny—it wasn't very hard and it seemed ridiculous that we hadn't done it before."

Based on the future of work in general and where her industry specifically was headed, Susan decided it was time for a major change.

"Once we figured out the future we wanted, it all seemed so obvious," she said. She then proceeded to fill me in on the details, in between bites of deep-dish pizza piled high with cheese and sausage.

After our coffee last winter, Susan became immersed in the contemplative stage of futurecasting, imagining the possibilities of what the future might look like. Her first step had been to expand her social network. It's easy for people in midcareer to get stuck in a rut since they've been surrounded by the same kind of professionals for so long. In Susan's case, that meant a lot of C-suite marketing types whose focus was always pinned to their company's bottom line.

She had started having coffee and lunch with people who worked at start-ups, nonprofits, NGOs, and other organizations she thought she might want to be involved with. The simple act of talking to people about the kind of career she wanted and the kind she wanted to avoid made the whole experience feel more real. It also allowed her to refine her ideal future career path.

"At a certain point in the process, maybe a dozen meetings in, I felt my whole life story starting to change," Susan said.

"You flipped the script." This is always such a gratifying moment when I'm working with a client. I often think it must be how psychiatrists feel when patients finally have that long-awaited breakthrough.

"Exactly!" Susan responded. "You know, I'm still proud of all the success I achieved in the corporate world. But I realized how little meaning I derived from it."

"Purpose over pleasure," I said, referring to our earlier conversations, and the teachings of Scott Cloutier, aka Professor Happiness.

"That's right," Susan agreed. "At first, it was scary to even contemplate a different kind of future, because the corporate salary has given us everything. Everything but purpose, that is. Once I flipped the script and made purpose the focus, a floodgate of possibilities opened up."

Within a few weeks, Susan's future had started to come into sharper focus. She knew that she wanted to use her experience leading major corporations to help others find their own pathways to success. She didn't want to start a company of her own per se, but she did want to help others launch and grow successful businesses. Above all, she wanted to help the next generation of female business leaders find their way in the world.

Now that Susan had a clear handle on the story of her future, she was ready to start workshopping it with other people. That brought her solidly into Step 2 of the process: identifying the future forces that must be harnessed to bring the future to life. Susan had never been a management consultant before, so she started exploring the various forces that would propel her to success.

She read books and articles and pored through case studies of people who had made similar career changes. And she continued to use her existing network and newly found experts to reach out to people she respected in her field. As she shared the story of her future with more people, she was encouraged by the positive reaction. A few colleagues even wanted to hire her on the spot, so good was her reputation. But she knew she had more work to do to make her newly imagined future a reality.

"All the meetings and conversations eventually led me to a mentor," Susan continued. "We've been working for the last couple of months on the formulation of a transition plan. This person made a similar transition herself, so with her guidance and support, I've been thinking along the lines of a consultancy firm that will only work with companies that I respect and that are committed to equality in the workplace."

"That certainly plays well with the future of work and the evolution of the gig economy," I said. "Plus, it's the kind of work you can do anywhere."

"Yes!" Susan shouted. "Patrick and I are already considering other cities to explore."

This work had taken Susan to the third and final phase of the process, the backcast, or determining the specific steps needed to bring her imagined future to life: the halfway, the partway, and the Monday. As Susan explained, the halfway phase of her backcast plan would involve building up credibility and expertise in the consultancy space by writing articles for outlets like Medium, becoming active on social media, and giving talks at conferences and other industry events.

To reach that goal, she'd first need to develop a point of view and body of work that she could use to promote herself. That would be the partway component of her backcast. Then there was the Monday, or the thing she could get started on right away to set her future in motion.

"I have a pile of research waiting for me at home, and I need to put together a list of conferences I'll try to speak at once I'm ready. It's all a work in progress," Susan admitted, "but now that I've given notice at the firm, I'm ready to hit the ground running."

"Excited?" I asked.

"Definitely," she answered. "And a little nervous. I'm happy I involved Patrick from the beginning. I don't know if I can make this future happen on my own."

"None of us can," I said. "Spouses, partners, friends, colleagues, the broader community—they all should be part of the decision process. I tell my students all the time, 'Life is a team sport.' And that's a good thing, because if not, life would suck and get pretty lonely."

"We're going to have to make some sacrifices financially," Susan said as lunch wound down. "But it will be worth it. So many people have said they can already see a huge difference in me. And why not? This is the future I always wanted."

TIME TO THINK LIKE A FUTURIST!

Quick Questions 2

There you have it, the futurecasting process. I can't and won't tell you your future, but through the strategies outlined in this chapter, you have the power and the tools needed to discover the story of your future, identify its various forces, and take the specific steps needed to get there. Susan's journey took her and her husband, Patrick, into a future that was both uncomfortable and exciting. The truth is that most futures are a combination of both.

So how will you apply the process? What futures do you

want to explore? Those are the questions that we'll tackle in the rest of the book. Quick Questions 1 was just a warm-up. This exercise is the first day at the gym, that first jog. There's no commitment; you are just testing the waters. There's still so much I want to tell you about the future, so I don't want you to attempt a complete futurecast now. But you are ready to start laying the groundwork by completing the following tasks. Take out your journal or device. It's the best way to turn abstract thoughts into actionable plans. Okay, here we go.

Part 1: The Future You

Write the Story of the Future You Want (or Don't Want)

Come on, you knew that was coming, right? You didn't think I was going to let you off with a softball. But relax. I don't want you to come up with the complete story of your future. For the purpose of this exercise, just focus in on one aspect. It could even be something relatively minor, like you want to take up meditation or join a book club. But try to be as detailed and specific as possible in the telling of this story. For example, what kind of meditation? Or, how many people are in the book club?

For the future you don't want, another way to think about it is to ask: "What am I good at that I don't want to do anymore?"

Maybe you are really good at something now but you don't want the future you to do it anymore.

The purpose of this exercise is to become better accustomed with the process. And details are everything when it comes to effective futurecasting. Pushing yourself to imagine the details will make the future you more real. The specifics also give you more material to work with when you're telling the story of the future you and identifying your future forces.

Part 2: Future Forces
Identify Five Forces for the Future You Want

In this part of the process, I want you to list your *people*, your *tools*, and your *experts*. You don't need to go all in and create a complete game plan around all three forces. But try to identify one or two future forces within each category. I'll use the meditation example as a jumping-off point for you to come up with your own more-specific questions.

QUESTIONS:

PEOPLE:

- **Do you know a friend or colleague who started meditating recently or made a similar life change, like learning poetry or the guitar?**

TOOLS:

- Is there a local meditation group you could attend?

- Are there any apps that could help?

EXPERTS:

- Are you aware of someone who has integrated the practice of meditation into their daily lives?

- Have they written a book or given talks?

As you are identifying your future forces, thinking through the details is just as important as it was in Part 1. Push yourself to get specific, writing down actual names of people or experts. List possible apps, groups, or other resources. This forces you to do a little work, but this work is already propelling your future.

Part 3: Backcast—
Sketch Out Your Halfway, Partway, and Monday

This final phase of the process employs the same mini drill. Think now about the incremental steps you will take to achieve your future. These examples of questions reflect the same meditation group idea, but again fill in your own, elaborating as much as you like on each backcast point in your proposed journey.

QUESTIONS:

- Is *halfway* when you have taken a class and feel like you can meditate on your own?

- Could *partway* be attending a class for the first time?

- Is *Monday* as simple as making a list of your possible future-force people and looking up possible apps and classes?

These examples are simple and straightforward, and that's very much the point. The purpose of this exercise is just to get you familiar with every step of the process so you can then apply it to larger, more complex challenges, like changing jobs or moving cities or finding love. Because I promise you, the same process applies regardless of what you're trying to futurecast. I've done it with Fortune 500 companies and I've done it with the guy at the end of the bar who's clearly going through a rough time.

So have fun with these exercises, but take them seriously too. As we move into heavier future topics, I think you'll see just how life changing the futurecasting process can be.

Up Next: The Things You Can Control

Speaking of heavy topics, control (or the lack of it, to be more precise) is something that weighs on many people, especially when it comes to figuring out their future. In chapter 4, we'll home in on areas where we feel particularly powerless, things like money, real estate, and planning. The bigger the issue, the less control we have. Or so we're led to believe. But as someone who routinely futurecasts massive, global, seemingly uncontrollable events like conflict, pandemic, and economic collapse, I've seen the process applied to just about anything.

You Have More Control Over the Future Than You Think

Now that you know how to think like a futurist, it's time to find ways to apply the strategy more broadly to your life. In order to do that, I want to drill down deeper into one of the core maxims of futurecasting, the notion that the future is built by people. Embracing this fundamental truth, with arms wide open, is essential to moving forward in the futurecasting process.

People's fear of the unknown, along with their sense of powerlessness over their future, prevents them from even contemplating how to change the future, let alone figuring out the steps needed to get there. They cling to the false belief that the future is fixed, when really nothing could be further from the truth.

People are the escape hatch from this self-defeating mindset. People build the future. Your future is yours to build. The power is yours and yours alone. You need to own this truth and take action.

Still don't believe me? Let me give you an example from my own life of how human beings build the future.

United States Patent #7673254, or What Steve Jobs and I Have in Common

Smartphones have changed the world. I don't think anyone would argue that point. With the power of a computer in our hands, this electronic device has affected nearly everything we do. It's changed how we connect with loved ones and get from point A to point B. It's streamlined the way we date and shop and find out what's going on in the world.

Go get your smartphone. Pick up this marvel of modern technology. Think back to the first time you ever touched one. It was like holding the future, right? I felt the same way—and I'm a futurist!

When you hold your phone, what do you think about? I've asked hundreds of people this question. Some tell me they think about the work they need to get done. Others wonder what's happening in their favorite social media app. A few people even talk about the embarrassment they feel over how cracked and dirty their screen is. But of all the times I've asked people what's going through their heads when they look at their phone, not a single one has ever answered, "I think about the thousands of people it took to build it."

I understand why. Who thinks about the people behind the devices we use every day? Smartphones are designed to look streamlined and cool and, above all, effortless to use. The designers don't want you to think about the tens of thousands of hours it took people to make it. They want you to use it and enjoy it. But when I look at my smartphone, I do think about the people behind it. Why? Because I was one of those people.

In 2007, Apple released its first iPhone, and it was an overnight sensation. Six million iPhones would go on to be sold in that first year of release. In major cities all over the world, lines stretched around the block outside Apple Stores with people wanting the thrill of being among the first to get their hands on the magical screen.

I want to show you a little something. Pick up your phone. Go into your contacts, where phone numbers and email addresses are stored. Start to create a new contact. When the blank screen comes up, press on the phone number tab, so that you can enter a new number. There! See how the keyboard changes from text and numbers to just numbers? That's my patent.

It's true. United States patent #7673254, with the catchy name "Apparatus, system, and method for context and language specific data entry." (Remember, I'm trained in engineering, not marketing.) The story goes back to 2006, a year before the iPhone's release, when I was busy designing new interfaces for electronic devices. Our team goal with this particular project was to come up with a way to have the fewest number of keys as possible on a small handheld screen. My solution addressed the problem in a clean, efficient way, so I put in for a patent, and now that little data functionality can be found on every smartphone in the world.

This is what Steve Jobs and I and thousands of other people you've never heard of have in common. We all worked in some capacity on the smartphone. We all made a small contribution that, when added up, resulted in a revolutionary device that's changed the way we live.

The same way I helped build the smartphone, as part of a team of thousands, is how the future gets built every single day. People build technology. People build the future. It happens step by step, bit by bit. Everything we as humans do ultimately comes back to people. Technology and business and commerce are part of it, but people are what drive the process along. That's why Step 2 in futurecasting—tapping into your future forces—is so important. Figuring out which people you'll need to help you build your future, and then connecting with them, gives you the information and momentum to turn the story of your future into a reality.

To further illustrate this principle, I want to bring up a topic that causes an inordinate amount of anxiety in people when they contemplate the future: money. Some of us worry that we won't have enough money saved for a comfortable retirement. Others take a more catastrophic view, worrying that they're just a job lay-off away from losing their home and ending up in bankruptcy court. Most of us land somewhere in the middle, unsure that we'll be able to put the kids through college or maintain the standard of living we've worked so hard to attain.

As you'll see in this chapter, these fears are easily laid to rest by recognizing that the future of money, and more specifically the future of personal finance, is all about people.

The People's Pundit

I always find going on live TV a little nerve-racking. I've done it dozens, if not hundreds, of times during my career. But I still feel my pulse quicken every time I set foot in a greenroom. The most anxiety provoking of all is live TV based in New York City that focuses on finance. The Big Apple is still the financial capital of the world, so it's a bit like talking politics in Washington, DC, or the movies in Los Angeles. Everybody's an expert.

On this day back in 2011, I was backstage at one of the big cable finance shows, about to do a live segment with a panel of talking heads. We were waiting for the stock market to close so we could see where the chips fell that day. This is the other thing about finance in New York City—it's always about the stock market. Who's up? Who's down? Where will the market close? Where will the market open? And why? Why? Why? Why? Entire careers are built and destroyed on the ability to answer those questions. But let's be clear: what everyone *really* wants to know is not what the market did today or why it did what it did. All they want to know is what that market will do tomorrow and how they can make money from that knowledge. In short, they want to know the future.

You can see why New York's finance gurus love to talk with me. The only problem is (as you now well know), I refuse to make predictions. I'm not an economist or an expert on financial markets. I will never make financial predictions, and it drives TV producers crazy. Still they invite me back to talk about the future.

So there I was that day, backstage, about to go out in front of the lights, powder all over my face and head. I've been bald for decades, and the makeup people always go to town dousing my dome in powder so it won't shine. It doesn't bother me, though it feels a little weird.

Four o'clock finally arrived, the closing bell rang, and it was time to go live. I was led out onto the brightly lit set where a team of analysts waited to chat about the future. I'm always struck by how intensely normal people look under bright studio lights. On TV they look polished and professional, but when you're walked out onto a set by an earnest producer in a headset, you look around and everyone looks like people you might see standing in line at the grocery store or seated next to you at church. They're just people. Smart people who can generally talk really fast, but just people nonetheless. I sat down on my swivel stool at the end of a line of four analysts and got ready for the segment.

"Hey, BDJ, how's the future?" asked Amir, one of the regular analysts. This wasn't my first time on the show. Actually, I had helped Amir write his commencement speech for his daughter's high school graduation in June of that year.

"Welcome back, BDJ," Janice, our polished host, said with a nod and a smile.

Fred, another analyst, chimed in, his hands clasped in prayer. "BDJ, what we really want to know is if the Yankees are going to win the World Series."

"You all good, BDJ?" Janice said over the banter. "It's the usual stuff today. We just want to hear about any new products and what you think is on the horizon."

"Sounds great." I smiled.

"Amir," Janice continued, "New Co. [not a real name] just announced they're laying off one-third of its workforce."

Fred pressed his earpiece, getting a fresh snippet of news from the producers. "Richard over at Thompson's [not a real name] just called in."

"Wow," Amir said, shaking his head. "You know that Kathleen at the *Times* is going to be all over that."

"This morning Sandy was on the show and said that the IPO was going to happen in December," Janice added.

"That doesn't look good," Fred said. "Can we get Sandy on the phone?"

This went on for several more minutes as I sat on my uncomfortable swivel stool waiting for my few supercharged moments on the air. In that instant, it occurred to me that here I was on the set of one of the most popular finance shows on television, and all anyone was really talking about was people. Yes, they were dealing with abstractions, like market rates and currency valuations, and how this all would affect the future, but really, when you got right down to it, the information was all about people. The future of money is about people. If you can find the right people, you can start to understand the future of just about anything. To put that another way, who you know is the biggest determinant of who you'll become.

With that lesson in mind, I'd like you to meet a guy called Maddox, to understand even more about how personal finance is a people game.

Finding the Cure for Indecision

"I want to have a conversation with you that I will completely deny ever having," Maddox said, leaning back in his metal folding chair on the convention floor.

It was October 2018, and I was in Boston for Founders Live, an entrepreneurs' event that moves all over the world. I had just come from one in New York, and the next event would take place in London.

What makes Founders Live so interesting is that you never know who's going to be onstage or, more important, who you're going to be sitting next to. I remember the first time I went to one I was sitting right behind former vice president Al Gore and former prime minister Tony Blair, eavesdropping as they debated the future of global business. You know, until you see Al Gore in person, you can't really appreciate how tall he is, or just how well he knows his facts. Though Tony certainly held his own that day.

Anyway, besides luminaries like Gore and Blair, at the Boston-based Founders Live event I also found myself sitting next to average-looking people who were doing extraordinary things. I met a college student who was working on her second start-up, aimed at transforming the way food is packaged. I chatted with a gentleman who was the chief investor in a collective of bankers looking for woman-owned companies to fund, because their math showed them that investment dollars went further when there was a woman in the CEO seat.

It was during an afternoon break in the action that Maddox came over and plopped down in the seat next to me with a sigh. He's a biologist-turned-entrepreneur I've known for several years. His newest company at that time was using synthetic biology to find a cure for cancer.

That's right, he is trying to cure cancer. Not exactly an underachiever.

"I'm serious, BDJ," Maddox continued. "I need your help. But if you try and tell anyone I ever talked with you about it, I'll deny it until the cows come home."

"I'm okay with that," I replied. "How can I help?"

"Well, I want to talk about money," he said in a hushed tone. "I want to talk about my money."

"You know I'm not a financial analyst," I countered.

"I know, I know," he said, shushing me. "I know all about what you do. I want you to talk to me about the future. How do I get my head and hands around what my and, more important, my family's financial future looks like? I figure if I go to a finance person, they're just going to try to sell me something. But not you. You'll just say you're not a finance person," he finished with a smile, slapping me gently on the side of the arm.

"You do know me well," I replied. "Should we go outside? It might be more private."

"Good idea. Let's jet," Maddox said, standing up. "We have thirty minutes before the next session."

"Oh yeah, sure, that's plenty of time to figure out your financial future," I said sarcastically.

We ventured out into the afternoon light. The sun was intense but felt good after a morning under artificial lighting. The air was just beginning to feel like fall, with a briny smell coming in off the harbor. We left the convention venue and strolled down to the water.

An Interview with an Expert:
What the Heck Is Money, Anyway?

A quick digression before we move on with Maddox's story. I want to talk for a moment about money. When I ask you "What is money?" your brain probably conjures up images of a one-dollar bill or the balance in your checking account. We all know money. We use it every day. We think about it all the time, including late at night, when we'd rather be thinking about anything else. You know those thoughts . . . *What if I lose my job? Is there enough for the kids' college? What if I get sick? Will I have enough to retire?*

To help with these late-night lashings, I want you to remember something: money isn't money. Money, like everything else, is all about people. Money couldn't exist without people.

To help you better understand this, I called on my favorite economist, Paul Thomas. (Yes, I have a favorite economist.) Paul and I worked together at the Intel Corporation. I was the chief futurist, and he was the chief economist, which made for many spirited water-cooler debates. He also had been the chief economist at Continental Airlines as well as a professor. But that's not why Paul is my favorite economist.

Over the years, I've worked with many economists, and what sets Paul apart are his unexpected insights and his sense of humor.

"So what the heck is money, anyway?" I asked Paul during a recent phone call.

"Well, you know, BDJ, there's a story about that," Paul began. "Economists like to tell it, which means there's probably no element of truth to it whatsoever, but it illustrates what money is quite nicely."

"Sounds great," I said.

"Supposedly there was this tiny island in the South Pacific," he began. "The people of the island decided they would each own shares in a set of rocks located just offshore. The more rocks you owned, the more money you had. They all agreed on the system and used it for transactions. But then one day a massive storm kicked up the ocean bed, and the rocks were covered with sand and debris. The islanders couldn't see the rocks anymore, and they all panicked. The money was gone! They had lost all of their money!"

"Fascinating," I chimed in.

"Don't worry, the story has a happy ending." Paul chuckled. "After a few days, the sand and debris were washed away and they could see the rocks again. Their money was back. The moral of the story is that money is nothing more than a notion of value that is agreed upon between people. The currency, the physical thing, doesn't matter at all. It's the agreement between people that matters."

Paul's point is an important one when you start thinking about the future of your finances. It shows the importance of people to the whole process. For me, I find it incredibly empowering that money is not money. It only has value when people agree to give it value.

Okay, back to Maddox. We were making our way down to the water.

"I'm supposed to be the genius," Maddox started. He's a big guy with a big personality, and a booming voice to go along with it. Even though he'd claimed he would deny ever having this conversation, I was pretty sure everyone on the block could hear us. (And in case you're wondering, he did eventually give me the okay to share this story here.) "I'm supposed to be the biologist wunderkind who is going to save the world from cancer, but to be straight with you, I can't even balance a checkbook. Doug isn't exactly a finance whiz either." Doug is Maddox's husband. They have two kids: Willa and Jeff, both in grade school at the time.

"I'm pretty sure there's an app for that," I joked.

"I'm serious, BDJ," Maddox continued, obviously not in a joking mood. "The future terrifies me. How do I make sure Doug is okay? What about the kids? We're gonna be talking college in ten years." Maddox ran his hands through his thick dreadlocks. "Ooph. I mean, how do I take control? I was freaking out last night, and Doug reminded me that your whole thing is looking ten years out into the future. Do you ever talk to people about this stuff?"

"Sure," I said. "I think I can help."

"Bring it on, BDJ," Maddox said, grabbing me by the shoulders. "Bring. It. On."

Ahh, the "Bring it on" moment—always my favorite part of futurecasting. It's like when you're out fishing and the big one first hits the line. Sure, there's still a ton of work to do reeling it in, but you know you've got 'im hooked. As Maddox and I continued our stroll along the water, my first task was to get him to think about a new financial future for himself and his family. Remember the key question from earlier: "What is the future you want?" That leads to a closely related second question: "What is the future you want to avoid?"

Maddox talked first and foremost about his fear of poverty, which is common enough but in his case was rooted in a destitute childhood, something I hadn't known about him. "Like eating government cheese poor," as he put it.

As a result of his upbringing, Maddox was crystal clear on the future he didn't want. Creating a story around what he did want was proving more elusive. "When you think about the future of your finances, what do you see?" I asked him.

"Fog," he answered. "It's all fog."

I wasn't going to let him off the hook that easily. As I explained in the previous chapter, it's so important to be highly specific when imagining the future you want. The more detailed a picture you're able to create, the more effective your futurecasting will be. If we'd been in his home or office, I would have locked Maddox away for an hour with a pen and pad and forced him to write down his future. Instead, I sat him down on a park bench and forced him to think hard about his future, for the first time in his life.

"And 'not poor' is not going to cut it," I said.

Maddox closed his eyes. Despite the bustle of tourists and business people streaming past, I could see he was seriously contemplating his future. I allowed my own thoughts to wander as well as I looked out over the shimmering waters of Boston Harbor. This stretch of water has always fascinated me, with its maritime past and fast ferries to nearby Cape Cod. A seagull honked overhead, eyeballing me to see if I was holding food.

Maddox opened his eyes and exhaled. "Okay, I got it," he said. "It comes down to two things. First, a house. I see us settled in a house that's a place for the kids to come back to from college and beyond. Number two: I want to make sure that Doug and I are set up for retirement, with something for the kids as well."

Real estate and retirement: they're two of the biggest planks in most people's financial portfolio, and they're also what gives us the biggest fits when it comes to the future. And why shouldn't they? The thought of growing old is scary enough. To also be homeless, or at least house insecure, *and* to have to scrape by on Social Security checks or meager savings, well, that's downright terrifying. Fortunately, the future isn't fixed, so no one has to succumb to this fate. I'll never say to anyone that taking control of the future is easy. And, indeed, it can be a good deal harder for people who have had fewer opportunities throughout their lives, whether because of financial hardship, family strife, or health issues. But even in those cases, a new future can be created. It starts by creating a clear picture of the future you want.

To See Yourself in Your Future House, You Have to Go Shopping for It Today

As Maddox and I made our way back to the conference, I got him to think more clearly about the kind of home he wanted for his family.

"You know, man, Boston is nuts," he said, shaking his head. "The prices are crazy, and they're only supposed to get worse. I mean, how am I supposed to prepare for that?"

This is a common pitfall in futurecasting. Before people even start the process, they're already psyching themselves out with all the reasons it won't work. My advice in that predicament is this:

take a chance on yourself. I'm not saying throw all caution to the wind or ignore the realities of your situation. If you're living on a schoolteacher's salary, maybe don't pin your future on a luxury penthouse. But don't be afraid to stretch your image of yourself. Remember my challenge from the previous chapter: dare to dream a different dream—a dream of a future that you really and truly want.

"Well, for starters, you need to make the future feel real and imminent," I said. "Go searching for it. Start looking for a house."

"We don't have the money," Maddox protested.

"Doesn't matter," I replied. "In fact, it's better that you don't have the money yet. When you do, you'll know what you want. It will give you and Doug a target, something to aim for. To see yourself in your future house, you have to go shopping for it today."

"That sounds like an advertising slogan," Maddox said with a sideways glance.

He was right. It did sound like a slogan. But just because a phrase is catchy doesn't mean it can't also be true. Our walk had taken us nearly back to the convention.

"Take a few weekends to look around," I continued. "You have to see yourself in the house. Don't fall in love with just one. Get to know what you like and what you don't. Get to know the prices. Talk with Doug about what you each want. Start to see yourself in these houses, and also in the neighborhoods. Give yourself the permission and the time to see that future down to the most minute detail. Heck, take a stroll through the local grocery store."

"Okay, okay," Maddox said. "I get the point." We made our way through the double doors of the venue and back into the conference.

"That will give you an idea of real estate prices and what you need to shoot for," I said, wrapping up the discussion. "Then comes the fun part."

"The fun part?" Maddox asked.

"Yep, then you need to find your people . . ."

Trade Secrets: How to Figure Out Your Number in Real Estate

I often have to remind people that my expertise is the future, and not in this or that particular industry. That includes real estate. I've bought and sold a few properties over the years, and even did well on the transactions. But that doesn't make me a real estate maven. Fortunately, there are plenty of mavens out there who can help you determine the specifics of your real estate future.

One whose advice I always value is Ilyce Glink, a syndicated columnist and author of more than a dozen books on real estate and finance, including the bestselling

100 Questions Every First-Time Home Buyer Should Ask.
Glink can expound on every aspect of the real estate
process, but when it comes to futurecasting, her best advice
is around determining how much house you can afford.
That might seem obvious, but according to one industry
report, roughly 40 percent of buyers go over budget on
home purchases by an average of twenty thousand dollars.

So how do you avoid this future? It starts by coming up
with a realistic budget, or "your number," as agents like
to say. Glink's website, ThinkGlink, boils it down to four
key questions that you need to ask yourself at the very
beginning of the house-hunting process:

- *How much money do I have saved for a down payment...?*

- *How much money do I take home each month?*

- *How much debt do I have?*

- *Have I researched costs in the neighborhood I want to live in? Can I afford them?*

*Liz Stevens, "How Much Can I Afford to Spend on a House?" ThinkGlink,
May 29, 2019, https://www.thinkglink.com/2019/05/29/how-much-can-i
-afford-to-spend-on-a-house/.

Coming up with clear, truthful answers to these questions will help you set a realistic budget in a neighborhood you can afford. The old rule of thumb was that your housing costs should be roughly 30 percent of your household's monthly budget. However, that ignores transportation costs, which can be significant if you have a long commute to work. And so it's best to add up your housing and transportation costs and make sure this total is no more than 45 percent of your household's monthly budget. There's a handy online tool called the Housing and Transportation Affordability Index (htaindex.cnt.org) that shows how affordability in nearly 220,000 neighborhoods across the US is affected when transportation costs are included.

These details are important to real-estate-based futurecasting because the effects of going over budget, to the point at which you run the risk of being "house poor," can be so debilitating. As ThinkGlink notes, "When families spend a higher portion of their income on housing costs, they spend less on other needs like healthy eating, exercise, preventative care and they're more likely to postpone medical or dental care. They're also saving less, if they manage to save at all, for emergencies and retirement."

*Stevens, "How Much Can I Afford to Spend on a House?"

I think we can all agree that this is precisely the kind of future you want to avoid.

Tapping Into the Future Forces

Maddox is not the kind of guy who sits on a project, so he wasn't going to let me leave Boston without finishing our talk. I agreed to grab a drink with him after the conference and explain every step of the futurecasting process.

"You need to find your people," I repeated as we settled on a plush leather sofa at a nearby pub. "Remember, finding a home isn't just about money and real estate. It's about people. The sellers, the buyers, the agents, the brokers. And the really great thing about all of these people is that they want you to buy a house."

"Okay, I'm with you," Maddox said.

"But wait, there's more," I said. "Once you've identified the people who will help you realize your future, next you need to search out the tools and resources that will help you reach your future."

"Like apps?"

"Sure, apps might be part of it, and also loan programs and savings plans," I said. "Again, I'm not a finance or real estate expert.

Your people will be able to help you identify these tools. Then there's one last group of people you need to pull together: the experts."

"Experts?"

"Yes, these are the people who have already done what you're trying to accomplish, whom you can learn from," I explained. "In your case, these would be people who have similar situations to yours—maybe someone with a spouse and a couple of kids who bought a house in the past and was successful at it."

"Gotcha, gotcha, gotcha," Maddox said excitedly.

"They could also be people who are experts in finding loans and researching neighborhoods."

"Makes sense." Maddox nodded.

Despite his enthusiasm, I could tell that Maddox was starting to feel a little overloaded. But I wanted to make sure I laid out the entire futurecasting process for him before skipping town.

"The final step is the backcast," I started.

"Wait, I'm going to have to start writing this down," Maddox said, pretending to search his pockets for a pen.

"I know it sounds like a lot at first," I said, "but that's because this is the first time you're hearing it. The process is actually pretty simple. Step 1: see yourself in your future. Step 2: find the future forces that will help you to get there, including people, tools, and experts. Step 3: work backward to determine the process needed to build the future."

"Oh, sure. Easy for you to say," Maddox balked. "You're the futurist."

"Don't worry. We'll get you thinking like a futurist in no time," I said. "With the backcast, it starts by plotting the specific things you need to do to get yourself halfway to your future. With buying a house, that might mean saving up a certain amount of money for the down payment. Once you understand what it means to be 50 percent of the way there, then you halve that again, to get you partway to your goal. In your case, this might be something like finding the neighborhood, identifying a few properties of interest, or establishing a relationship with a banker or mortgage broker."

"Makes sense." Maddox nodded.

"Once that's all done, you determine what you need to do Monday, to officially start the process."

Maddox let out a big bellowing laugh. "You make it sound all so easy," he said. "But the truth is, it does sound doable! Now that I actually know what to do."

"That's awesome!" I said, raising a glass to toast his future. "I want to hear how it's going in a few weeks."

The Family That Futurecasts Together . . .

"I hate grass," Maddox said suddenly, after a long, contemplative silence.

"What's that?" I asked. I wasn't quite sure I'd heard him correctly. We were sitting on the small balcony of his apartment in Boston. It was about eight months since we'd had our chat along the harbor, and the air was unseasonably warm. I was in town for a few days, and Maddox had insisted I come over for a Sunday barbecue. Grilling out on the dinky balcony of their rental apartment was a little ridiculous, but I think Maddox wanted to do it to push himself along in his quest for a home. Doug and the kids were inside, waiting for the dogs and sausages to finish cooking.

"I hate grass," Maddox repeated. "This is something I never knew about myself. I mean, who hates grass? I never really thought about it, but it turns out, yeah, I hate grass. In fact, I hate all yard work."

"I am completely lost." I smiled. I was used to being lost in conversations with Maddox.

"I followed your advice, BDJ," he said. "Doug and I went looking at houses so that we could see ourselves in our future. That's how you put it, right?"

"Yes, that's right," I said. "Go on."

"Yeah, so we looked around and found a few neighborhoods we like, got an idea of prices and all that stuff we talked about. Then it turned out we have friends, another couple with kids, who have a house in one of the neighborhoods we were looking into. They would be experts, right?"

"Yes," I replied.

"So this couple was going on a monthlong vacation, and they knew we were interested in the neighborhood. We had talked to them about the future we wanted." I could tell he was trying hard to use the language of futurecasting. "They asked if we wanted to house-sit for them so that we could get a feel for the neighborhood. We were able to make it work with the kids' school, so we took them up on the offer."

"Wow!" I erupted. "That's awesome. What a great way to actually try living in the future you want. So cool."

"Yeah, I thought it would be great," Maddox said, proud of his work. "We stayed in the house. Loved it. Loved the neighborhood. Loved it all except for one thing."

"What's that?" I asked.

"The house had this huge backyard," Maddox said, his voice growing dim. "We were excited to barbecue and let the kids run around out back." He motioned to the pitiful little grill at our feet. "And it was great, until the time came to cut the lawn and take care of the yard. 'Cause that's what homeowners do, right?"

"Oh no," I said. "I think I see where this is going."

"Yeah. Turns out, yard work sucks," Maddox spat. "I hate it. Doug hates it. I think even the kids are allergic to grass. It was horrible. Horrible!"

"That's awful." I chuckled, imagining Maddox's misery in the backyard. "But it's good you found it out now."

"I know!" he agreed, bending down to check the dogs.

"So what's your future now?" I asked.

"No grass," he said quickly. "No backyard at all, unless it's a patio."

"Seriously, though," I said, pressing for details. "What's your future look like now, what's halfway and partway? Because it sounds like you accomplished Monday."

"Oh, we are really far along," Maddox said, waving me off.

"We've done all the stuff. We have *people* now . . ." He had emphasized the word to make a point. "We have a realtor keeping an eye out for us. We have a mortgage broker and a financial planner."

"Wow! That's great. Have you—" I started.

"Slow down, future boy," Maddox interrupted with a smile. "Let me give my full report before we go back inside. I think we hit partway last week. Our savings and investments have been moved around, and our finance person knows the goal is a townhouse." As he talked, he moved his hands in the air like he was arranging boxes. "We should hit halfway in the fall, depending on a few things with work. You know, curing cancer and all is tough."

"That's a lot of progress," I said, trying to be as encouraging as possible.

"Oh, there's more," he said. "Doug loves futurecasting. We sat down as a couple and then we sat down with the kids to talk about the futures that we all wanted. We futurecasted as a family!"

"The family that futurecasts together . . ." I started.

"Don't give me another slogan," he said, transferring the dogs and brats from the grill to a serving dish. "We're also working with our financial adviser on where we want to be in the next five to ten years."

"Maddox, this is incredible," I said, clapping my hands. "You really did it. You really made amazing progress."

"Thank you, BDJ," he said, his voice growing serious. He looked me square in the eye. "No, really, BDJ, thank you. I feel so much better, and our harbor talk seems so long ago."

"You're welcome." I nodded. "It's a pleasure."

"But you better be careful," he added, opening the sliding glass door to the apartment. "My kids are futurist-mad right now. They're going to hammer you with questions."

"I can't wait," I replied. And I really couldn't.

THE POWER OF PEOPLE
Quick Questions 3

Okay, back to the questions . . .

Whenever I say that to my students, they know it's time for an exercise. This is a good moment to hit the pause button in the chapter and apply the connection between people and the future to your own life, within the broader context of the futurecasting process.

Instead of starting you out with three questions in this exercise, I want you to come up with three people you believe could play a role in helping you create a positive future for yourself. We all have these people in our lives, individuals we respect and admire and gravitate toward, because we know on some level that they could be a positive influence. The operative word there is "could." Because even when we recognize the value a person could bring to our life, too often we fail to act.

Why is that? I think it's because we haven't thought enough

about the future we want and how this person could be helpful in attaining it. Remember, the worst thing you can do in life is allow—or expect, even—someone else to determine your future. That includes waiting for someone you respect to tell you what you should do with your life.

In the first part of the exercise, you will identify three positive people in your life. In the second part, you'll figure out a specific part of your future you think they can have a role in, and how the relationship might play out. In some respects, this exercise might feel like simple Mentoring 101. But it adds in the critical futurecasting layers by forcing you to think in very specific terms about the future you want and how these individuals can help get you there.

I like to do this exercise in my own life at least a few times a year. In chapter 1, I told you about Andy Bryant, one of my mentors at Intel. He was one of my *people*. When I was interested in doing futurecasting on a more individual level, he was critical in helping me figure out what that might look like. He challenged me. He asked me hard questions, questions that I didn't know the answers to and needed to go think about for a while. But it was that uncomfortable conversation, not knowing and taking the time to reflect, that led me to seeing my future in a more concrete way. That conversation changed my life. It showed me a new, clearer version of my future.

Another one of my people, a person who propelled me, and continues to propel me, toward the future I want and the person

I want to be, is Tiana. If I look at the two of us, she and I couldn't be more different. We have different backgrounds, life goals, worldviews, and experiences. We often don't agree, but her perspective and participation are vital for me to craft more complex and inclusive futures. She almost always starts off our conversations by telling me why I'm wrong, how I've missed something, or the perspective I'm lacking. But the discussions are positive and constructive, with the goal of making the future better.

Okay, now it's your turn.

QUESTIONS:

- **Who are three (or more) people who will play an active part in the creation of your future?**

- **Who can help propel you to the future you want?**

- **Why do you think they can help?**

- **Will they support you in a positive way?**

FOLLOW-UP QUESTIONS:

- **Do these people have an alternative perspective to yours?**

- **Do you and these people come from different backgrounds?**

- **Will these people challenge you?**

In addition to answering these questions, as a bonus revisit Quick Questions 1 for yourself and then take it to the people you have identified. Ask them the exercise questions and use the questions to have a conversation about the future. See how that discussion goes. Was it positive? Did you feel more energy and support after the conversation than before it started?

After you've taken the time to reflect on Quick Questions 1, go back to your people and tell them about the future you and that you'd like to involve them in this process. I bet you'll find they consider it an honor and are willing to do what they can to make your future come true.

A View from the Bottom

Before we move on from people and the future, I want to share one more story to show how this critical shift in perspective can lift people from the lowest depths of despair.

I was sitting in my library, writing a research report, when I got a text: "You there, futurist?"

"Yep," I replied. "What's up?"

"Tell me I have a future," Tara answered.

I'd met Tara at a town hall I had participated in that explored the future of technology and the American dream. The event had been held on the campus of Iowa State University in Ames, Iowa. That was a few years ago, and those years had not been kind to

Tara. She had experienced some mental health issues, which had then spiraled into financial troubles.

"You have a future," I texted.

"I have $300 in my bank account, rent is $1,100 and it's due in two weeks. Tell me what I'm supposed to do with that future?"

"Call me when you can," I replied quickly. "Let's talk."

Tara had reached out to me about a month before. She had filled in the gaps since we last met on the campus of the university. We had chatted a few times about her future in general, but I hadn't realized it had become this dire. What Tara didn't know was that I was familiar with the view from the bottom.

I'm comfortable having these conversations. Turns out I know a few things about having limited resources, feeling financially helpless, and living down to your last penny.

In August of 2001 I was a founding member of a technology start-up. It was a technology that I had a lot of faith in, and my work as a futurist pushed me to believe that there would be a melding of the internet with TV. This was long before the iPhone, long before the smart TVs I would build with Intel. I really believed.

Because I believed, I dumped all of my savings, credit, and assets into the company to help get it off the ground. Then 9/11 happened. With the economic slowdown that followed, all the investors we had lined up for our little company pulled out. We went broke. I lost all my money and eventually had to file for personal bankruptcy. I know what it means and how it feels to be at the end of your rope.

That's why I will always take calls from people who, for whatever reason, find themselves in a hole. I've been in a hole too, and so I might be able to help find the way out.

My phone rang.

"You must be frustrated," I said calmly.

"Yes and no," Tara replied. "Yes, I feel frustrated, thank you." I could tell she was trying to be polite, but fear and frustration were gnawing at the edge of her voice. I could tell she wanted to scream and yell, but she knew it wasn't appropriate. "But I also feel fed up, you know? I mean, sure I've made some mistakes and some missteps, but does that mean my whole life will be like this, wondering how I'll even pay rent?"

"I don't think so," I replied. "It won't always be like this. There is another side to your current situation."

"Really?" she said, again with an edge of anger in her voice. "I just feel powerless and worthless, like I have no worth in the world, like I will *never* have any worth ever again."

Tara was starting to spiral. Powerlessness, frustration, and fear have a way of amplifying one another, sending you deeper and deeper into the abyss.

"What can I do to help?" I asked.

"You could give me a thousand dollars," she replied quickly. Then after a moment she said, "No, BDJ, I'm not calling you to ask you for money. I mean, if you did want to give me a grand it would make my immediate life a lot easier, but that's not your gig. I know that."

"So what can I do to help?" I asked again.

"Tell me something," she said with a heavy sigh. "Tell me I have a future. Give me some hope."

"You have a future," I said flatly.

"Funny." She laughed. "I already got that text from you. That's not what I meant."

"I understand what you meant," I said, cutting her off. "I'm telling you that you do have a future. There is an ending to the present you. You will get to the other side of this. But I want you to tell me: what's the future you want?"

"A thousand dollars," she answered.

"What's the longer term future you want?" I asked. "Can you see yourself in a different future?"

"I can't even imagine the end of this week," she replied.

"Well, try," I urged. "Try to see yourself in a different future. One where you aren't scared about making rent. One where you feel like you have some power over your situation."

The line went silent for a while, a deep, dead silence. I let it hang there, giving Tara space. It had been a long time since someone had given her the permission and the platform to imagine a future different from the panicked present she found herself in.

"Ugh, okay." She sighed. "If I'm honest, I think I want to go back to school. That's where I made my big mistake, where I derailed myself. I know all the reasons why I did it. I panicked. It's the gift of being bipolar: I'm the maestro of panic. I won't bore you with the details."

I knew many of the details.

"So yeah, I want to go back to school. But I'm so broke now, I could *never* get back to Ames, and I really don't want to live in Iowa anymore. I'm staying in Virginia. Again, I won't bore you," she said, starting to spiral again. "It's just impossible."

"It's not impossible," I replied. "You did it once before and you can do it again."

"But how can I afford it if I can't even make the rent?"

"We aren't talking about your present right now," I answered. "I understand that your situation is bleak. But go with me for just a few minutes. I won't make this long. You have more control than you think. You will build your future."

"Okay, I'll play along," she agreed.

"Where do you want to go to school and what do you want to study?" I asked.

"Honestly, I don't care where I go," Tara answered. "Just being able to go. And I'd like to finish my degree in physical therapy. I do miss that."

"Great," I continued. "Next we can figure out how to get you there."

Just like with Maddox, we talked through the details of Tara's future forces. When we got to assembling her team, the conversation really hit a nerve.

"Who are the people who will help you move toward schools, toward the future you want?" I asked.

"I don't have anybody," she said quietly.

"People who will help you get to that future," I prodded.

"I don't have anyone," she repeated. "I've alienated my family, and for sure my ex-husband will never help me ever again." Her voice cracked.

I didn't know that Tara had been married. She had never mentioned this.

"There are many, many people who can help," I said, trying to bring her back.

"Like who?"

"The people at the school you want to attend, for starters," I explained. "You can go and talk with them. They could be people in admissions or financial aid or even community outreach. It doesn't cost anything to go and visit the college and meet the people who can help you get there. It might sound simple, but it's a great initial step."

Tara was quiet for a time. "You mean like just go and talk to them? Why would they talk to me?"

"They want to talk to you," I answered. "It's their job."

"Huh," she said. Something had changed. The edge had lifted from her voice. "I see what you mean."

We continued talking about her halfway and partway plans.

"Listen, BDJ," she said finally. "I've already taken too much of your time, but I get it. I see what you mean. I mean, I still need to get myself together and pay rent, but you know, just seeing that different future and being able to talk to people who want to talk with me about that future makes it feel real, like I *can* do it."

"You can do it." I smiled.

"You are an optimist." She laughed. "But I appreciate the support."

Tara did figure out how to make rent. She also set up a visit to Old Dominion University in Norfolk, Virginia, near where she was living. They have a good physical therapy program, and she found plenty of people to connect with. That was her partway. Last I heard, Tara was about to reach her halfway, enrolling in a night class at the university with some help from the financial aid office.

Up Next: More Than People Build the Future

Like Tara, and like Maddox and his family, you have the power to imagine, design, and bring about the future you always wanted. By seeing yourself in the future you want and taking specific steps, bit by bit, conversation by conversation, you will make that future happen.

Embrace the idea that people build the future. You will build your future and the future of your family, your business, your community, and whatever else you choose. Identifying the people who can help will propel your future into reality.

There is one more key element to learn when you are future-casting your life. Over the years I have discovered that the future is not just built by people. That takes us to another key maxim of futurecasting, and the topic of our next chapter: the future is local.

CHAPTER 5

The Future Is Local

The future is built by people. Hopefully I convinced you of that fact in the previous chapter. Now I want to move on to another core truth of futurecasting: the future is local. What do I mean by that exactly? When I speak to general audiences, I answer that question by posing a different one: "Where do you think the future is being built at this very moment?" Most people imagine a sleek, shiny laboratory in Silicon Valley. Or the corridors of power in Washington, DC. Or some faraway factory in China. Rarely do they allow for the possibility that the future is also being built every day right in their own backyard.

And yet that's the logical next step in the theory of futurecasting. If the future is built by people and people exist in physical locations, then all futures must be local. To come at that another way, futures are created when passionate people get together in a room, roll up their sleeves, and get to work realizing a shared vision. The room might be an actual physical space or it might be something virtual, say a video call or a social media platform.

The key thing is that in order to build your own future, you need to be in the right place at the right time. On the face of it, that might seem obvious. But I can't tell you how many people I meet whose futures are on hold because they're in precisely the wrong place to move their lives forward. It might be that their career is stalled because they're in the wrong industry. Or they can't find love because they're living in the wrong city. Or their health is failing because they're stuck in the wrong social circle, leading the wrong kind of lifestyle.

In order to create a new future for yourself, you first need to change the story you're telling about it. As part of that process, you also have to ask yourself where this new future is most likely to happen and then take the necessary steps to get yourself there. I'm now going to tell you about a few people who did just that.

A Whole Life Ahead, but No Future in Sight

Random texts come with the territory of futurism. My phone often buzzes at odd hours of the day and night with messages from contacts I haven't heard from in months, if not years. It's no bother. In fact, I take pride in being a kind of lifeline for people in need. People like having a futurist on their speed dial. I like to imagine them uttering the old *Who Wants to Be a Millionaire?* game show phrase "I'd like to phone a friend" as Regis Philbin obligingly gets me on the line.

So it was late one weekday when a text message came through from an old contact named Jon. He worked as an agent at a large insurance company, one I'd been consulting with for several years in my private practice. We'd gotten to know each other over work dinners, baseball games, and other social outings.

"Can you talk?" the text read.

"That's ominous!" I responded, then: "Yep. How 'bout now?"

A few seconds later my phone rang.

"Hey, Jon," I answered, trying to tamp down any hint of worry in my voice.

"I hope I'm not crossing a line here," Jon began with a sigh. "It's just that when she said it in the first person, I thought of you right away."

"Wait, what's happening here?" I said. "Is everything okay? Because you don't sound okay."

"Sorry to be so cryptic," Jon answered, doing his own best to not sound worried. "It's my daughter, Roxanne. I'm not sure what to do."

"How can I help?" I asked.

"She's been going through a rough time," he explained. "She just graduated from art school and she's completely lost."

"That can be a hard time for young folks," I said.

"It's more than that, though," Jon said. "Last night over dinner, she said there was no future. That *she* had no future. That's when you popped into my head. I know we don't know each other well outside of work, but I was hoping you'd be willing to talk with her."

This wasn't the first time a worried parent reached out in need of a mentor. "I'd be happy to," I told him, and we made arrangements to connect.

The Enchanting Power of the Overwhelmingly Obvious

The video-call icon sprang to life on my phone, chirping away, waiting to be answered. I was in my library in the Pacific Northwest, calling Roxanne in Minneapolis.

"Hello, it's BDJ," I said, as the call connected and her video screen booted up.

"Oh, hi. Thank you," Roxanne replied hesitantly. "My dad said that we should talk." She was seated at what looked to be her parents' kitchen table, in her early twenties with close-cropped hair and a bull-ring piercing in the septum of her nose. I don't normally focus on a person's appearance, but I couldn't help but also notice a striking tattoo of a Bengal tiger on her neck. The tail and back legs came up from her right shoulder and the head was under her chin near her right ear.

"It's nice to meet you, Roxanne," I started.

"Call me Rox." She smiled. "Everyone does."

"Okay, Rox," I said, shifting in my chair. "How can I help?"

"My dad says you're a futurist," she said quizzically. "What is that?"

I launched into my spiel about futurism, explaining the work I've done.

"Yeah, okay, I guess that makes sense." Rox nodded. I was some old dude her dad told her to talk with, and her skepticism was running high.

"Your dad mentioned you're thinking about your future," I said.

"No." Rox smiled, glancing up at the ceiling and back at me. "I told my dad that I feel like I have no future, and he freaked out." She began to relax the more she talked. Her candor and honesty were refreshing. "I just graduated from college. I have a mountain of student debt. I still live at home with my parents. I don't want to keep going to school. I actually want to work, but since I graduated I really haven't found anything that I'm passionate about. So from where I'm sitting, yeah, the future doesn't look so bright."

"Have you gone on any interviews?" I asked, trying to get a better handle on her situation.

"Yeah, some, and I even got a job at a local construction firm here in Minneapolis," she explained. "It's only been a couple weeks. I work in their marketing department, doing 3D modeling and character animation, which is what my degree is in."

I imagined Rox with her nose ring and tiger tattoo in a Minneapolis construction office, then checked myself, becoming suddenly aware of my unconscious bias and the fact that I was filtering what she said by who I *thought* she was.

I had made up a story about Rox before she had fully told me her story. That's bias in all its ugly glory. Even though I really wanted to help, I still fell into that trap of listening through a filter.

We all use filters when we speak. When we speak to kids we filter. When we speak at work we filter. When we speak we say specific words and leave others out.

But we also use filters when we listen. When we make assumptions or think we *know* a person, that becomes hardwired into our brains. We only *hear* them as *that person*. Even if that person changes or takes a different point of view, we will still hear them as we think we know them, not as they really are. We cannot actually hear and understand what they are saying. On one level I had robbed Rox of her individuality. She was a complex person I didn't know, and I had already started assuming things. I needed to step back from this, be aware of it, and push myself to remain open.

When you find yourself filtering, hold yourself accountable. Look for the best and react to the words that are being said, not what you think those words really mean. Listen to the words and take action from there.

"So how can I help?" I asked.

"That's a good question," she answered. "How *can* you help? Dad says you help big companies and militaries, but of course I'm neither." Her tone was fascinating—not rude or impatient, but oddly frank and to the point. She seemed to defy every expectation that I and possibly most of the professional world had about her.

"Well, the method can apply to anything." I smiled. "Anyone can think like a futurist."

"Okay, futurist, go for it." She nodded.

"What kind of future do you want?" I began. "And what kind of future do you want to avoid?"

"The answer to that seems overwhelmingly obvious, doesn't it?" Rox said, thinking aloud in her matter-of-fact tone. "I want to work in animation, just not for a construction company. I want to get out of student debt. I *really* want to get out of my parents' house. Yep." She nodded again, with a somewhat sly grin. "That's pretty much it."

"But where is that future?" I pushed. "You want to work in animation and not live with your parents. So . . . where exactly do you want to work? Where exactly do you want to live?"

"I—" she started, then stopped. Her mouth hung open for a moment, then clamped shut like a trap. She rubbed the tail of her tiger tattoo absently, then started and stopped again.

"How 'bout this, Rox," I said, breaking the silence.

"No, futurist," she said, holding up her hand. "Let me sit with this." She sat a moment and then said finally, "Oh, I don't know. I've never thought about the future this way before."

"Everybody's future is local," I told her. "For many people, understanding where that future is and what it looks like is the critical first step toward achieving it." I watched for some flicker of recognition, but her gaze was pitched stubbornly off-screen. "Once you figure out the where, there are specific steps you can take to get there," I added.

More tortured silence.

"Okay, I'm in," she said suddenly, snapping her attention back to me. "Give me a week."

"Great!" I said, not exactly sure what had just transpired.

"Okay, futurist, bye." She waved with both her hands. "I'll text you with some times next week." Then she hung up.

What an interesting young woman, I thought.

If You Want to Be a Lumberjack, You Need to Move to the Forest

"Hey, futurist," Rox said the following week, her now-familiar face filling my screen. There was something different to her voice. It was at once less guarded and less confident.

"Hello, Rox," I said. "How was your week?"

"Crappy," she answered. "How many dual-use live-work buildings can a girl model?"

"I don't know, how many?" I laughed, trying to put her at ease. "So did you have a chance to think about—"

"Yeah, yeah, yeah," she interrupted, waving her hands in front of the camera. "I want to work at Pixar."

"Pixar?" I asked.

"You know, the animation studio that made *Toy Story* and *WALL-E* and just about every other animated movie worth watching."

"That's great," I replied. "I know Pixar. I don't think I know anyone there, but have you looked to see if they're hiring?"

I was going to continue but stopped as Rox leaned in close to the camera, one eyeball filling the screen.

"Are you okay?" I asked.

"I'm watching you, futurist," she said, leaning back in her chair again.

"For what?" I asked.

"You didn't laugh," she said. "I thought you would laugh. A professor at school smirked. And Andy, the girl I sit next to at the office, she practically busted a gut she laughed so hard. But you didn't."

"Why would I laugh?" I asked.

"Because I'm a kid from nowhere Minnesota, with no money and an art degree from some rinky-dink liberal arts college," she said, shaking her head. "How am I going to get a job at the most important animation studio in the world?"

"Now, that, Rox, is a great place to start our futurecasting journey," I said.

I've described this scene before—the "game on" moment when a client moves from a kind of contemplation phase about the future to being ready to take the plunge. Rox might have been plagued with self-doubt as we talked, but I could tell there was a part of her that was starting to believe this new story of her future. That's an important lesson in futurecasting: doubt, disbelief, naysaying—these are often signs that the future is near. If there's a voice in your head saying, *That will never work*, or if someone else is saying it to you, that's often the moment to double down on the idea. That's the course I took with Rox.

"Who are the people who can help you get there?" I said, diving headfirst into the futurecasting. In her first week of work, Rox had completed Step 1 of the process, coming up with a bold new future for herself, working as an animator at Pixar. Now she had to identify the future forces that would propel her toward that future. "Who are the people who have done this kind of thing before?" I asked her. "What tools and resources are out there? Who are the experts who can help you?

"You want me to call John Lasseter?" she replied flatly. "You know, the director of *Toy Story*."

"You could try that." I shrugged. "But you may want to start a little further down the food chain. Meanwhile, are there local professional groups you could connect with? Maybe networking events geared for people looking to break into animation."

"So what, I'm supposed to hop on a flight to California, make my way to Emeryville, and start hanging out with animators?"

"Well, if you want to be a lumberjack, you need to move to the forest," I said.

As you know by now, I'm a man who loves a good maxim, and this is another one of my go-tos. I realize I've been saying since the start of this chapter that the future is local. But that doesn't mean the right future for you is happening in your own backyard. Some futures you have to move to. Rox was obviously not happy working for a construction firm in downtown Minneapolis. She was working in animation, just not where she wanted to be.

"You're like a lumberjack living in the Great Plains, surrounded by prairie, nary a tree in sight," I said. "So yes, Rox, you have to move."

"You're bonkers," Rox said, pawing at her tiger's tail. "I don't have any money. I don't have any time. I can't just up and move."

I had fully expected this reaction. As I've said many times, futurecasting is hard work, and it often involves dramatic life changes, like relocating across the country. That's where the backcast comes in. It's designed to make the monumental feel more manageable. You find the halfway point, then the partway, then the Monday. Rox had been a quick study at figuring out the new story of her future. Now it was time to slow things down and help her take the first step.

"You don't have to move," I answered. "Not right away, at least.

You visit first. You meet people. You network. Who knows? You might even find out that you don't like the West Coast."

We got into the nuts and bolts of traveling inexpensively, like keeping an eye out for flash bargains on airlines that fly to the West Coast. Because Rox had the flexibility to travel at off-peak times, she could get to California for a lot less than she realized. Next we brainstormed places she could stay, including with friends of friends.

"I just remembered, my college roommate has a sister who lives in Emeryville," Rox said. "She used to crash in our dorm all the time. I bet she'll put me up for a few nights."

Rox's Monday was already filling up. In addition to the travel logistics, she would need to start lining up experts who might be in a position to help her, using enabling technologies like LinkedIn and Glassdoor. Were there people from school who might have an in at Pixar or other companies related to animation? Even massive industries have smaller subsets of people who tend to know one another. Rox needed to worm her way into the right group, maybe by looking for an industry event she could attend while she was on the West Coast. Then she needed to prepare a list of questions to ask her experts the moment she was given the chance: "How did you get your start?" "What is a typical day like for you?" "What are the biggest challenges?" "What are the things I need to be doing to prepare myself?"

As we were wrapping up the call, Rox confided, "I really

thought you'd laugh at me." She wasn't looking at me. Her attention was fixed on a list she was writing. "This is bonkers," she said finally, looking up.

"I think you can do it," I replied. "Your to-do list comes first. That's your Monday. Partway is finalizing the trip, including meetings and a possible networking event. Halfway is when you start applying for jobs based on recommendations from the people you meet."

"You make it sound so easy," Rox said.

"It's not easy," I replied. "But it is doable."

"Okay, futurist," she said, waving at the screen. "I'll text you sometime from the future." The screen went blank.

As Promised, a Text from the Future

Rox's path to her future was not a short one. Her dream was big, and anything big takes time. Over the next year, I checked in every few months to see how her progress was going. Rox was extremely methodical with the process, connecting with other animation professionals, finding the people who could help her. These people connected her with experts, many of whom generously gave of their time for informational interviews.

She went on to discover that Emeryville was just one city in an entire region of the West Coast, from Los Angeles to Portland, where the kind of work she was interested in was being done. As Rox learned more of the ins and outs of the business, she also discovered that animation stretches far from the world of Pixar. Nearly every shot of most medium- to big-budget movies is touched by an animation or special-effects technician. From fixing little flaws on a film set to adding backgrounds and altering buildings, their input is never-ending.

The lack of immediate gratification didn't bother Rox. I was worried that she might become discouraged or lose motivation. But having a long-term goal and specific steps to take each week and month made the work and the wait more bearable. And it made her less disgruntled about her job—no more dark jokes about no future worth living for.

I was pleased to learn that when Rox told her boss at the construction company about her hopes and dreams, as well as the steps she was taking to make them a reality, he was supportive.

"He said he never really thought I'd stay that long," she told me during a quick check-in chat. "He actually said everyone there knew I was destined for something bigger."

After her second trip to California, I started to hear less and less from Rox, though her dad assured me things were going well. Then one day he emailed to let me know that Rox had gotten a job—not at Pixar but at a smaller animation studio in Los Angeles.

A few months later, I finally got that text from the future.

"When you see the new Marvel movie, don't leave at the end!" Rox wrote. "Sit through the credits. You'll see a name you recognize in the second to last animation studio credit. Mine! Bonkers!"

"Not bonkers at all," I wrote back. "Welcome to the future."

The Keys to Finding Your Local

Rox's story shows the extent to which all futures are local. It also underscores how important where you live is to who you are and who you will become. Too many people take a passive approach to the decision, allowing it to be made for them, instead of finding a city or town that suits their personality and ambitions. When thinking about the correlation between place and identity, there are certain geographical affinities to consider, for example that introverts prefer mountainous terrain while extroverts gravitate toward beaches. These are generalizations, of course. There are plenty of chatty people in the mountains and bookworms on the coast. Nevertheless, often where you live has some influence on who you are as a person. And so when I work with individuals, I always encourage them to think about the importance of place when coming up with the story of their future.

One significant question to ask yourself in this process is how much you value family time. This of course assumes you have a relationship with your parents, siblings, and the like. If you do and you're close emotionally, you might be reluctant to move far away. And I respect that—as long as you've fully considered what that future relationship will look like. It's comforting to think about parents being close by, maybe to help take care of your kids, if or when they come along. But is that really going to happen? Or might they not be as helpful as you hope, leading to resentment, especially if, in your heart of hearts, you know that your future is somewhere far from the family nest. Think hard about close relationships in your life and how you want them to play out in the years and decades to come.

On an equally practical level, you need to think about whether you want to rent or own your home. You can do either in most parts of the country, though buying a home will be much harder in pricey real estate markets, like New York, Boston, and San Francisco. Even if you can afford your home, ask yourself if it fits with your future career and lifestyle. Some jobs allow, or even require, you to move around a lot. That could be harder to manage if you have a home to care for, versus an apartment where all you have to do is lock the door on the way out.

Then there's the question of passion. I know a guy who is a massive sports nut, follows every major sport and a lot of the minor ones too, and he moved to Hartford, Connecticut, one of the biggest US cities without a major sports team. I told him not to do it. He didn't listen. Six months later he quit his job, broke his lease, and hightailed it back to Boston. The moral of the story? If you love something—sports, music, hiking, theater, whatever—make sure where you live will support the passion. Otherwise, you run the risk of a miserable future.

One final practical consideration when thinking about place:

How much do you travel? Traveling could be a passion, but it might also be a job requirement. Either way, if you're going to be on the road a lot, live somewhere that will make it easy to get up and go. Proximity to a major international airport is key. Topeka, for example, is nice in many ways, except for the seventy-five-mile drive to Kansas City International Airport.

Happy Hour: A Brief History of Futurism

As long as we're on the subject of place, I thought I'd take a quick detour into the origins, and evolution, of futurism. Throughout my twenty-five years in the business, I've collected a cast of colorful, not to mention incredibly bright, characters. These are the experts I call on for insights on a range of subjects, from economics to politics to social sciences. When it comes to the topic of futurism itself, my go-to is a guy called Greg Lindsay.

Greg is officially an urbanist, specializing in the future of cities, technology, and mobility. Beyond that, he has the deepest understanding of the history of futurism of anyone I've ever met. He also happens to be the sharpest-dressed guy in the biz—putting the "urbane" in urbanist, as I like to say. I've never seen him without a tie. He was even wearing one when he sent me from the hospital a picture of himself with his new baby. Whenever we get together, there's always a bit of the Odd Couple to us, with Greg in his bespoke suits and polished shoes, and me in my blue jeans and beard.

That was very much the case when we last got together in New York City, soon after I started in on the research for this book. Greg and I had talked before about the origins of futurism, our chosen career, but I wanted to get the complete story once and for all. I was especially interested in hearing more about futurism's somewhat controversial past, as well as how Greg was feeling about the future of futurism. Greg's mind is amazing. He is a two-time *Jeopardy!* champion and the only person to go undefeated in a game against IBM's supercomputer Watson. Over martinis at the Bemelmans Bar, in the Carlyle Hotel on Manhattan's Upper East Side, we went deep into the future.

"When I talk to people about the history of futurism," I began, "I think almost everyone is surprised that it started as an art movement. At the beginning of the twentieth century the term 'futurist' was mostly applied to poets and artists. Why do you think the story starts like that?"

"The beginning of the twentieth century was a time of extreme and rapid change," Greg explained. "Just after World War I, the world modernized really quickly. The future seemed all around. It makes a lot of sense that artists were leading the way, because they were imagining a different future. The future wasn't this old, stodgy thing. It was new and exciting and full of promise."

The bartender dropped off some nuts and made sure our glasses weren't empty.

"Then there's another shift after World War II," I said, popping some peanuts into my mouth.

"Yes, that was a dark time," Greg said, adjusting his jacket. "It was the Cold War. Futurist think tanks were being asked to imagine a future after nuclear war—or worse, after mutually assured nuclear destruction."

The businesswoman sitting next to Greg at the bar must have heard a snippet of our conversation. She glanced at Greg with a puzzled look, then returned to her conversation.

"But during that time, in the 1950s and 1960s, we also saw the rise of private futurists," Greg continued. "They started consulting and working with large corporations. The profile for futurists as a profession was on the rise."

"And then the Tofflers happened." I smiled.

"Yes." Greg nodded, amused by my enthusiasm. "Then the Tofflers happened."

Alvin and Heidi Toffler were a husband-and-wife team who popularized futurism, bringing it into people's living rooms. Their 1970 book *Future Shock* was wildly popular. When I was growing up, it seemed like everybody's parents had a copy. As a young geek, the futuristic cover always grabbed my attention. The book described the rapid acceleration of technology and its effect on culture and business. The couple even made a documentary about it, starring none other than Orson Welles.

"You met them," I said, egging Greg on. Back in 2010, as part of the fortieth anniversary of *Future Shock*'s publication, he met the couple for an article he was writing about how the book was still applicable today.

"There's a part in the book where Heidi talks about clothes made out of Kleenex," Greg said, glancing up at the ceiling. "That seems kind of silly, but she pointed out to me that it's an example of what we today call 'fast fashion.' Cheap clothes that aren't meant to last long. Their take on consumer culture is still applicable today."

"Why do you think the '80s were such a bad time for future thinking?" I asked.

"Yeesh, yeah," Greg said, steeling himself with a sip of martini. "It was the dark ages for futurism. The discipline was boiled down to trend reports and dumb taglines searching for the next hot color in women's dresses. Everyone was looking for the next big thing and wanted to make sure they were the one who told you about it first." Greg shook his head. "The future was commodified and sold, and people got rightly skeptical."

"I saw the next change begin in the '90s and really as we moved into the twenty-first century," I said. "The PC and the internet started to speed up business. People started seeing small start-ups get big quickly and turn into billion-dollar businesses. Corporations and organizations saw the potential and the threat of not looking into the future."

"You also can't downplay the fall of the Soviet Union and the Berlin Wall," Greg added with a nod. "Up until then most people thought that at some point in the future there would be an end to the Cold War stalemate . . . in the form of a nuclear war. But when the wall came down suddenly there wasn't just one future, there were a bunch of possible futures. Anything was possible now. The world wasn't going to end in fire. The future was unlocked."

We finished our martinis, and the happy hour business crowd started to thin out, replaced by couples and tourists getting ready for a night at a Broadway show.

I motioned for the bill and asked, "Last question . . . What's the future of futurism?"

"Ah, the question everyone likes to ask." Greg rubbed his chin dramatically. "You'll know that answer as much as I would, but I'll tell you what I'd like the future of futurism to be."

"Yes, please." This piqued my curiosity.

"Ultimately, I think futurism shouldn't be just for governments, militaries, and large corporations." Greg leaned back, scanning the room. "It should be a way for communities and groups to come together and envision a tomorrow that they want to live in. I think it should be for people, average people, so that they can build their future."

I got the biggest smile on my face.

"What?" Greg asked, a little worried by my grin. "Too corny?"

"Not at all, my friend." I reached out, shook his hand, and slapped him on the shoulder. "You couldn't be more right. That's the exact reason I'm writing this book."

Finding Your Future (Partner) in Your Hometown

As I've been saying throughout this chapter, the future is local. Rox had to move to a place where the future she wanted could be found. If you want to be a lumberjack, you move to the forest. But that doesn't mean everyone has to relocate to achieve their future. Sometimes you can find it in the town where you live.

To demonstrate this, I'll tell you about one of the more uncomfortable experiences I've had in my career as a futurist. We're now going to talk about the future of love and relationships and finding your future mate.

Starting Over in the Sunshine State

I've told you how often my phone buzzes with random texts from the past. This one read: "I saw you're coming to town. Can we talk? I'll buy you coffee."

This was from Ruth, a banker I'd worked with from time to time when I was looking at the future of money and emerging financial technologies. I hadn't heard from her in quite a while. I knew Ruth was going through a divorce. I also knew it was a particularly nasty split, which unfortunately does happen to good people. There was a son in college, various properties and assets, plus a whole lot of animosity.

Among mutual acquaintances, Ruth's breakup was the kind of subject people didn't like to talk about. The divorce had dragged on for a long, long time, and whenever anyone brought it up, the news was bad, unfortunate, and, most of all, deeply unsettling.

Eventually I started to hear that Ruth was finally on the back side of the whole thing. She'd found an apartment in Orlando, new work, and was starting to get her feet under her again. It just so happened I was going to be in Orlando speaking at a conference.

"Yep," I replied to her text. "Name the place."

As long as I live, I'll never get used to Florida humidity. I've spent most of my life in the Pacific Northwest, where there's little humidity. Ruth remembered this about me and said we might as well meet at the coffee shop at my hotel in downtown Orlando, to spare me from having to walk outdoors. I like Ruth a lot.

• • •

The lobby bustled with business people glad-handing, chatting aimlessly, and checking their phones. All around me I could hear deals being done or planned, along with the usual office gossip. When a six-year-old girl in full princess garb skipped through the sea of suits, it was like catching a glimpse of a unicorn. She was obviously fresh from a trip to Disney World and still levitating from the sheer joy of it.

Ruth spun through the revolving doors and quickly spotted me.

"BDJ," she said after a quick hug.

It was great to see her, though to be honest, she looked a little worse for wear.

"Hey, Ruth," I replied. "Thanks for meeting me here. How are you?"

"Not as terrible as before," she answered. "I'm sure you've heard all the dirty details of my shambles of a life."

"Actually, not all of them," I said, more or less honestly. "Just bits here and there. I heard you got an apartment in Orlando."

"Yes, my one-bedroom sanctuary," she breathed. The way she'd said "sanctuary" sounded like both a blessing and a curse.

"No, really, it's great," she said, perking up. "It's lovely. David, my son, he's up at the University of Florida. I like being close to him."

"How's he liking Gatorland?" I asked.

"You know what?" Ruth said, placing her palms on the table. "I didn't drag you down here to talk about this. How about I go get us some caffeine and we can dive in?" She grabbed her purse and raced to the counter.

"Okay," she said a few moments later, setting down the beverages. "Here's the thing, BDJ. I've been through some stuff."

"I think that's an understatement," I said.

"Well, yes," she said with a genuine smile that relaxed us both a bit. "A few weeks ago I was sitting in my little apartment thinking, for the first time in a long while, about what was next. And a question popped into my mind. It was so clear, clearer than anything I've felt in a long, long time."

"What was it?" I prodded.

"What's the future of love?" Ruth said. She paused for a minute, blowing on her tea before taking a tentative sip. "Not only that—what's the future of love and relationships and marriage and sex? You're the futurist, you should know."

My head began to spin. The chattering business types suddenly grew irksome. What was I supposed to say?

"So that's my question, mister futurist," she said. She was more relaxed now, as if she had transferred her anxiety to me. She was free.

I, on the other hand, was freaking out. Ruth had obviously been thinking about this for a while. It was the path out of the confusion she'd been living in for some time. I didn't want to get it wrong. I took a breath and said, "You want me to tell you the future of love and marriage and sex? Is that the big, capital-*F* Future, like for everyone? Or are we talking about you?"

"Good point," she said. "Both!"

A sip of coffee, then the final admission: "I can't help you."

"What?" she said, shaking her head with a strange kind of satisfaction. "You mean the futurist can't answer my question?"

"I can't," I admitted, holding up my hands in defeat. "I can't help you. This is not what I do. I'm not an expert in this area. I wouldn't know where to start. Plus, I'd be terrified of getting it wrong. What you're asking me, Ruth, is a really big question."

"I know it's a big question," she said, banging her palm on the table. "That's why I'm asking you. If anyone could know, it would be you. Can't we use your process? Can't you just try?" She reached across the table to grab my hand.

"I . . ." I started, looking down at her boney hand. Her grip was intense and desperate. But it was also the hand of a mother. I honestly think she was more worried about me in that moment than herself. I looked up at her face, and I got the exact same read from her expression as I was getting from her hand. "Okay," I said, glancing downward again.

"You'll do it?" she asked.

"Yes." I nodded. "But understand, I'm not an expert in this area. I can walk you through the process, but as with any kind of futurecasting, I won't have the answers. That will be up to you."

"I'm in!" she said, letting go of my hand. "Let's do it!"

"Not now," I said, slowing her down. "I will need a little time to prep. I'm here for a few days at the conference. Let's talk on Friday afternoon before I fly out. We can have a nice long lunch and talk it out."

"I'm about to explode with happiness." Ruth beamed.

"That's good, I think," I said, taking another sip of my now luke-warm coffee and wondering what exactly I had gotten myself into.

Bring in the Anthropologist!

I went back up to my room and quickly emailed my go-to social scientist, Dr. Genevieve Bell. She's a social anthropologist, technologist, futurist, VP, and all-round intellectual badass. We literally worked side by side at the Intel Corporation (the cubes were small), finding ways to make computers more human, emotional, and meaningful.

Bell is still a senior fellow and VP at Intel, as well as a professor at the Australian National University in Canberra, Australia, where she grew up. As her bio page at the College of Engineering and Computer Science says, she's busy "exploring how to bring together data science, design thinking and ethnography to drive new approaches in engineering" and "exploring the questions of what it means to be human in a data-driven economy and world."*

I fired off a message: "Quick question: what's the future of love, marriage, relationships, and sex? Also . . . hope you're well!"

As expected, she delivered immediately.

"Well, you know me," she began, "I always start with the literature—Robin Fox, David Schneider, Kath Weston, Helen Fisher. Start with a steady diet of anthropologists." Over the years, Bell has been the source of some epic reading lists. Always insightful. Always interesting. "From there," she continued, "I would want to remind your client that relationships, kinship, marriage, and even love don't always work the same."

"How so?" I asked.

"Well, there are all different kinds of love," she answered. "There's romantic love, love of family, love of God, love of country, even love of products and possessions. What's the love you're talking about? Figuring that out will help to shape your future. Just remember everything is on a spectrum."

I understood what she meant. Love, marriage, relationships, and sex are all on a sliding scale, meaning that people define them differently. Each is an individual concept, and so how you define it is uniquely individual. This is evident in the fluidity of gender

* Data61 CEO Adrian Turner, speaking of Genevieve Bell's return to Canberra, in "World Leading Technologist Dr. Genevieve Bell Returns to Join ANU," news release, ANU College of Engineering and Computer Science website, January 27, 2017, https:// cecs.anu.edu.au/news/world-leading-technologist-dr-genevieve-bell-join-anu.

and sexuality that's become more accepted in recent years. How each person defines their gender or their sexuality can be wildly different. This applies to relationships, love, marriage, and sex as well.

For example, when I say the word "sex" to you or "making love" or "sexual relationship," the image that will typically pop up into your head speaks to your sexual preference—the person you prefer to have sex with. If I say "marriage," the same thinking applies. You will see the type of person you are or want to be married to. More broadly, when I say "relationship," you can see a whole continuum of relationships. This is what Dr. Bell was getting at. You might see a love relationship or a relationship with your parents or your children (if you have them). Or you might think about your relationship to your god or religion.

Applying this idea to Ruth would be interesting. Her understanding of love and marriage and relationships had been rocked by her messy breakup. As a result, she was reluctant to make the same mistake. But would she be unable to imagine a different kind of love, leading to a different kind of future? The point was that there isn't one type of love or relationship or sex. The future of love is less binary than what Ruth experienced the first time around. I thought that might liberate her from her fears and allow her to imagine a different and better future for herself. But it would also challenge her. She would need to examine who she was and the future she wanted.

This can get messy when we're talking about love, relationships, and sex. People discover things about themselves that make them uncomfortable or that they're not ready to accept. But it's important to remember that there is no right answer. There is no one way to be. There is no right way to be. There is just you and the future you want.

After a few days of keynotes and Q&As at the conference, I was ready to take this step with Ruth. We decided to meet at the hotel again for a late lunch.

The Superpowers of Jewish Grandmas

"Hello, BDJ," Ruth said, giving me a big hug. The dining room was empty, the throng of business people having migrated elsewhere. We had the room to ourselves, except for an elderly couple eating by the windows overlooking the pool. Kids splashed around while parents sunned themselves and chatted idly.

"Okay!" Ruth started. She looked like a woman transformed. The slumped shoulders had been replaced by an eager enthusiasm.

"Before we start, let me remind you," I said, pointing at my bald, bearded head. "Not qualified at all to be having this conversation with you. I'm here to help. But not qualified."

"Yeah, yeah, you already said that," she replied with a wave of a hand. "Where do we start? Tell me my future." She pretended to be squinting into a crystal ball.

"So I went to an anthropologist friend with your question," I said, then relayed Dr. Bell's insights, including her proposed reading list. I told her that everything was on a spectrum, and she needed to decide where she was today and where she wanted to be in the future. What kind of love are we talking about in the future? What kind of sexual relationships? It was nonbinary, meaning it wasn't either-or, one or the other. There was a whole range of possibilities, and the right answer was up to her.

"Well, that certainly gives me a lot to go on," Ruth said once I had finished. "And it broadens the possibilities for the future. What next?"

"Well, the first step is to ask yourself what kind of future you want," I said, diving headlong into the futurecasting process. "You have to see yourself in the future you want. In so doing, it's sometimes helpful to ask yourself what is the future you want to avoid."

"Ha!" she cried, slapping the table with her palm. "I can tell you that. Witness the last twenty years of my marriage. Actually, that's not true." She paused. "It wasn't all bad. The last ten years, let's say. That will work."

I glanced over at the gray-haired couple, with the chaos of children in the pool in the background. Watching them pick at their salads with relaxed smiles centered me.

"That's a great start, but we need more detail," I continued. "What is the future you want? What does the future relationship look like? What do you want from it?"

"I don't know," Ruth said, shaking her head.

"I usually find a good place to start is with experts in the field,"

I said. I picked up my phone and did a quick search of "What makes a healthy relationship?" The internet is often a mess. I always tell people not to ask the internet a serious question. But that day it was surprisingly sane. Here are a few of the top results to the query:

(from a dating website)

Mutual respect

Trust

Honesty

Support

Fairness/equality

Separate identities

Good communication

A sense of playfulness/fondness

and (from a wellness website)

Respect

Equality

Safety

Trust

and (from a psychology magazine website)

Respect

Nonthreatening behavior

Trust

Support

Honesty

Fairness

Economic partnership

Shared responsibility

Responsible parenting [if you want to have kids or dogs or cats or fish . . .]

After reading the various lists, I said, "When you think about the future relationship you might want, those are some pretty good places to start. They are simple traits of a healthy relationship."

"Yeah, I can work with that." Ruth had started to take notes. "Heaven knows my last relationship didn't have a lot of these qualities by the end."

"It gives you a framework to think about what you want from your future love/relationship/marriage/sex relationships. You'll need to answer those questions for yourself and see what that relationship would look like. But you also need to ask yourself, 'Who?'"

"Who?" she said.

"Yeah, who do you want that relationship to be with?" I treaded lightly into uncharted futurist territory.

"What if the answer is 'I don't know'?" she questioned.

"That's okay for now," I said. "But for me to help you figure out what comes next, you will need to know. I can't help you until you answer that first question."

"Okay, let's say I have answered the first question," Ruth said. "What comes after that?"

"To better help you understand your future, you need to ask who are the people in your life who can help propel you toward the future you want," I said. "Who is your team?"

"My team?" she balked.

"These are generally family members or friends who can help you realize the future," I continued. "They're people you can tell your future to and they'll support you or even help you out."

"Like a Jewish grandma!" Ruth blurted out.

"What?" I knew that Ruth was religious and Jewish, but I wasn't sure what she meant.

"Come on, BDJ," she chided. "There's a long history of Jewish grandmas being matchmakers in the community. Remember *Fiddler on the Roof*?"

"Oh, right," I replied. "I guess that does apply here. Sure, why not? So to repeat: your 'people' includes anyone who will listen to your story and provide guidance and support."

"Got it," she said. "What's next?"

"Tools and resources," I answered. "They can be people too, but more often they're organizations or legislation or technology that can help."

"Dating apps!" Ruth blurted out, like a contestant on a game show.

"Yes." I sighed. "But, you see, here's where I feel I can't help. I met my wife before the internet and dating apps took off. Who am I to tell you what your best resources might be?"

"It's the Jewish grandmas!" Ruth said excitedly.

"Huh?"

"I'm thinking about my synagogue and the social meetups and functions that go on each week. They're meant to bring people of faith together to have conversations. It's so much easier to chat with someone you have something in common with."

"Agreed," I said.

"And these events are run by—wait for it—Jewish grandmas! BDJ, I think I cracked this thing wide open. What's next?"

"Experts," I said. "You need to find experts who have gotten to the future you want and who can give you insights into how to get there."

"You know what I'm going to say, right?" Ruth smiled.

"I think I do," I answered.

"Jewish grandmas!" she exclaimed. "Okay, now I know the future I want and the things that will get me there," Ruth said, without any loss in enthusiasm. "What's next?"

"The backcast," I said. "What are the steps you can take to get halfway between where you are today and where you want to be? Then halve that again and figure out what it means to get partway there. Finally, ask what you need to do Monday to get started."

Ruth took notes furiously. "I know you think I'm making fun of this, but I'm really not," she confessed. "I'm sure that the super-powers of Jewish grandmas will figure into this somewhere, but I now see what you mean. I see what I need to do."

"That's wonderful," I said. "Any more questions?"

"Nope," she said, snapping the top back onto her pen with a flourish. "I have a lot of homework and thinking to do. And you, my friend, have a flight to catch."

I checked the time. "That's right, I do need to get going."

"Don't worry about the check," Ruth said, standing up and motioning to me. "Come here and let me hug you until your face explodes."

On the plane ride home, I replayed the conversation with Ruth. It wasn't surprising that the future of love, relationships, and marriage is all about people and that it's local. Ruth had seemed to get inspiration out of our chat. The process had provided clarity and a way to approach her questions. Futurecasting gives people a framework to see their future and what they need to do to get there. It also makes the process seem doable and less daunting.

Giving a person relationship advice still made me uniquely uncomfortable, but I kept telling myself that it wasn't me who was going to answer Ruth's questions. I wasn't telling her the future of love, relationships, marriage, or sex. I was simply providing a map.

• • •

I didn't hear from Ruth for some time. I got pulled into my private-practice work, and I assumed she too was occupied with business and family. To be honest, I think I was a little scared to reach out and see how things were going. I didn't want to mess things up or make her situation worse. So for a time, not knowing anything felt better. Plus, this was Ruth's personal life. Reaching out to someone and asking about their job search is different from asking about their love life. But eventually I did reach out.

"Doing great," Ruth replied via text. "Our chat was a huge help. Thanks and hugs!"

That was it. But that was enough.

A few more months went by, and I didn't hear anything more. From friends and social media I could see that Ruth was active and out and about in the world. Then, as summer was approaching, I got another text out of the blue.

"Hey, BDJ, sorry for the silence. Thought I just wanted to be alone. Guess I was wrong. Am going on a date this Friday. Jewish grandmas strike again. Yikes!"

It was followed up by one smiley-face emoji and one scared-face emoji.

"That's wonderful," I replied quickly.

"This is my partway . . . I guess . . . first date [another scared-face emoji]. You were right . . . if you want to meet people, you have to go to where they are . . . Met him at my synagogue . . . volunteering . . . Wish me luck!"

"Good luck!" I wrote back.

Throughout the summer, I heard nothing. As Ruth receded from my life, I began to feel that this was the right thing. It was her personal life and it should remain that way. I didn't have any other role to play. I'm sure if there was, Ruth would reach out. There was nothing more I could do to help, and that was enough for me.

As the holidays approached, I caught sight of a few pictures of Ruth smiling and posing with the same gentleman. He was about her age, with salt-and-pepper hair. I remembered that first afternoon in Orlando and the weight that had seemed to push down on Ruth's shoulders, plus the exhausted expression in her eyes. Seeing Ruth's current smile and her anticipation of the coming holidays gave me all the resolution I needed.

"Awesome," I said out loud to myself and went back to my research.

THE THINGS THAT HOLD US BACK

Quick Questions 4

Let's take a break and apply some of this local future talk to your own life.

"Local" is a relative term. Rox needed to pick up and move across the country to find her future. Ruth, with the help of her posse of local Jewish grandmas, simply needed to search around Orlando to find the future she desired.

For Quick Questions 4, I want you to focus on a current barrier to your desired future. What are the things standing between you and the future you? You can think about these barriers in terms of the stories and themes covered so far in this chapter, like work or love. Or topics covered in previous chapters, including where you see yourself living and what kind of financial situation you want to be in. Or they could be smaller in scope—say, hitting some target of physical health or becoming adept at a certain skill.

Once you've identified a barrier, or a few barriers, answer the following question:

QUESTION 1

Where is this particular barrier to your future right now?

In some cases, the answer to this question will be obvious and fairly focused. If you want to be a country music star, you go to Nashville. If you want to study marine biology, you head for the coast. Other times, there will be multiple paths leading to your future place. I think romance is like that. If you're young and single, growing cities will have a high percentage of eligible partners. But as Ruth's story showed, you can also find love in your own backyard, if you know where to look. So there probably won't be one right answer here. I just want you to think hard about where you need to be to find the future you're looking for.

FOLLOW-UP QUESTIONS:

- **Where did the barrier come from?**
- **Do you have control over that barrier or will you need help from your future forces to remove it?**

Don't forget the details. The more you can describe the thing separating you from your future, the easier it will be to move past it.

QUESTION 2

What/who are some future forces that will help you get past the barrier?

This is another opportunity to practice the process. Don't worry about checking every box and formulating a complete plan. But write down a handful of forces—people, tools, and experts—that might be helpful in this part of your journey. Remember the fundamentals. A good team member is someone you can bounce your idea off of and who will respond with honest, constructive feedback—say, an old bandmate from college who spent time in Nashville herself. Tools can be sources of deeper information—maybe an online dating app tailored to your specific interests or a local program that could help. And experts have already done what you're looking to do—perhaps a marine biology group on LinkedIn where you can learn about career prospects once you earn your degree. In this same manner, come up with five forces of your own that will help lead the way.

FOLLOW-UP QUESTION:

- **Do you have ready access to your future forces (people, tools, experts)?**

The people here should be the team that surrounds you in your life. Your team is local. But the tools and experts can come from anywhere.

QUESTION 3

What specific steps can you take to move around that barrier?

This is backcasting. We're not looking for a fully formulated plan. I just want you to start to work these mental muscles. What's the halfway point to where you want to be? Scale is a factor here. If achieving your future involves a cross-country move, there are going to be many more steps than if the answer is in your own community. Don't overthink it. Remember, the point of the backcast is to take a process that feels too hard and overwhelming and break it down into manageable parts. Rox freaked out when I first presented her with the idea of moving to California because she felt like it was all going to happen at once. In fact, the process involved multiple steps taken over many months. I realize this in and of itself can feel daunting. But the more you do it, the more patient you become, releasing the need for instant gratification that's so ingrained in our culture. You start to appreciate the journey, seeing it as its own kind of reward.

FOLLOW-UP QUESTION:

- **Is there a barrier that feels too large to move? Can it be nudged?**

Seeing the Future by Saving the Past

There's one more kind of local future I want to tell you about: your local community. How do you make the future better for your community and the local people around you? In my private practice, I've had the opportunity to help local leaders figure out the future they wanted not only for their organizations but also for the communities they serve.

I'm often called upon to help when a business or organization is in crisis. It's rare for the CEO of a successful, high-performing company to wake up one morning and say, "You know what? Let's bring in a futurist!" It's happened once or twice, but companies and individuals usually reach out to me when they realize they aren't prepared for the future. Very early in my career I had to get used to tough conversations and tense situations.

One winter I received a call from the board of directors for a small history museum in Michigan on the shores of Lake Huron. A board member had seen me speak at a conference on science and history museums. Yes, there are a few of those out there, and I have a weakness for them. (Believe it or not, I was even married in a planetarium.) So when the call came in, I wasted no time in making travel plans to the Great Lakes.

Winter had come early to Michigan. There was already a few feet of snow on the ground when I arrived, and it was supposed to snow again before the end of the week. The desk manager at my little hotel joked that I didn't need to worry because they never close down the local airport unless it gets really bad, and really bad in Michigan is different from the rest of the country.

"But didn't they just say on the TV that it was going to be really bad?" I asked.

"Yeah." He shrugged. "Thought maybe I'd give you a little hope."

I didn't know how to respond to that, so I just replied, "Thanks. Have a good day!"

"Yep," he said with a wave.

The museum was set on the shores of the lake, with a wide deck that stretched out over the water. Recent renovations to the two-story building gave it a fresh and welcoming presence. I sat in the small café with the incoming and outgoing chairs of the board. The room was so cold that I kept on my hat and scarf, but the lake views were breathtaking.

"We don't know what we want," said Nadine, the incoming chair, shaking her head. She was the one who had seen me speak, and she was eager to get the museum's future on track during her tenure. "We're doing way too many things, and most of them don't make sense."

"Don't make sense?" Dan said softly, without a hint of confrontation. Dan was the outgoing chair. "The museum's membership is higher than it's ever been."

"I just think we're doing too much, Dan," Nadine pressed. "It's not sustainable."

Obviously Nadine and Dan had different visions of the museum's future. To make the situation more complicated, the two could not have been less alike.

Nadine was a local real estate broker and developer. Her business card actually read "Nadine, Nadine, the real estate machine." Throughout my whole time working with the museum, I never saw her dressed in anything but a perfectly tailored business suit.

She was precise, successful, and driven. And part of her drive was aimed at giving back to her community.

Dan was a botanist and a retired professor from the University of Michigan. He had a fondness for open-toed sandals and well-worn fleece pullovers that were embroidered with the names of obscure scientific conferences. By his manner, I could tell that he had spent a lot of time by himself observing delicate woodland fauna. His love of nature, learning, and the local community formed the purpose of his golden years.

That was really the only thing these two had in common: their love of their local community and a desire to make it better for the future.

"Do you know what kind of future you want for the museum?" I asked them. "Or more important, what is the future you want for the local community? The future is always local. I think if you can answer that question—figuring out the future you want for the community—then it might help you have a better understanding of the role the museum can play."

"That's a good point." Dan nodded.

"But we already have a charter that tells us the future we want," Nadine answered. "We exist to preserve and share the history of Lake Huron and the people it touches."

"That's a great start," I said.

"Then why do we run day-care services Monday through Friday?" Nadine responded.

"Because we need them," Dan replied. "When Tiny Tots Day

Care closed down last year, there was no place for families to take their kids. Plus, many of the moms couldn't afford Tots in the first place."

"But free day care for the community isn't in our charter," Nadine said.

"We have the space for it," Dan said, pointing to the second floor. "We have the staff—"

"But what does that have to do with preserving and sharing the history of Lake Huron?" Nadine repeated, her tone getting a little more heated.

Dan was still as cool as a cucumber. "It has to do with preserving our local community," he said.

"It sounds like there's a mismatch of purpose," I said, jumping into the debate.

"That's why you're here," said Nadine.

"The first step is for you two and the board to develop a vision for the future you want," I started. "Talk about the future you want to avoid as well. Then we can figure out the museum's place in it."

"How do we do that?" Dan asked.

"There are a couple of steps to start," I said. "First, the board needs to get in a room and do some serious futurecasting, as a group. Getting passionate people together to develop a shared vision can be powerful."

"We can get that scheduled," Nadine said, picking up her phone.

"Hold up," I said. "I think you might need to do part of Step 2 before you do Step 1."

"What's that?" she asked, looking up from her phone.

"Well, typically when I do this with people I have them envision themselves in the future they want. Then I have them look for the people, tools, and experts that can help propel them there. But in this case, I think you should start by talking to the people and experts first. I also think it would be helpful for you to hear from the community about their wants and needs."

Nadine and Dan both stared at me blankly. I could tell they were processing.

"That sounds like a lot of work," Dan remarked finally.

"It is," I answered. "But anything that matters takes work, especially when your goal is to make the future better for an entire community."

"The board isn't afraid of hard work," Nadine said, turning back to her phone.

"You two, the board, your volunteers and staff, you all have a unique opportunity in front of you," I said. "It's rare when people are given the permission and the platform to think about the future and then start acting upon it. You're in a position to truly make the future here better."

For Nadine and Dan, the next few months were hard, but they both told me individually it was some of the most rewarding work they'd done in a long while. The museum started a series of listening sessions and town halls to hear what the community wanted.

Members of the local government, school system, and city services chimed in. They hosted fun events for kids and talked with the parents and caregivers over ice cream and coffee.

I was impressed with their diligence and passion. Nadine was right: the board wasn't afraid of hard work. Plus, once they had identified their people and experts from other science and history museums who had evolved to meet the needs of their own communities, they were leaps and bounds ahead for their backcasting.

I returned in early spring, a lovely time to visit. The chill was finally out of the air, and tiny wildflowers were just starting to peek up through the ground.

I sat in the same large café with Nadine, overlooking the calm waters of the lake. We were waiting for Dan to start. The next day I was going to run a futurecasting session with the board in the morning and then one with the local community in the afternoon.

"We still have the day care," Nadine said, staring out the window.

"Is that a good thing?" I asked.

"Did you know that I was a single mom?" she asked, still looking out the window.

"You never mentioned it," I answered.

"Yeah," she continued. "I won't bore you with the details, but there was a stretch a long time ago when it was just me and my son. I was on assistance, like so many mothers we help here."

"It must feel good to be able to help them," I said, urging her to talk more.

"It does and it doesn't," she continued. "Of course it's great to be able to help. But it doesn't because I was so fixated on the charter and what our mission as a museum should be." She looked me smack in the eyes. "I'm a rule follower if you haven't noticed."

"I've noticed." I chuckled.

"I don't know, I think it was a mismatch of futures, to borrow your term," she continued. "Those listening sessions really helped me explore the future I want for the community. To tell you the truth, BDJ, I'm not sure what our place is, what the museum's place is in that future, but I'm really excited to discover it."

"That's great," I said.

"It really is a big opportunity," she said, her gaze drifting back out the window. "Maybe one of the biggest in our lives if we get it right."

"BDJ!" Dan yelled as he entered the room. I had never heard Dan speak in anything but hushed tones before. He came up to me and gave me a big bear hug. His fleece sweatshirt read: UNIVERSITY OF ESSEX BOTANY EXPO, COLCHESTER, UK.

"Hello, Dan," I said, patting him on the shoulder once he had released me. "It's good to see you."

"I'm so excited for tomorrow." He beamed. "Has Nadine been telling you all the amazing things she's been up to? Of course not—she's too modest. Well, let me tell you, the board has been transformed by this project. Connecting with the community and understanding the future we want have given us new purpose.

Our volunteer numbers are through the roof. People really want to help."

"Then you're already on your way to Step 3, figuring out the backcast process that will lead the community where it wants to go," I said.

"We owe it to Nadine and all her wonderful ideas," Dan said.

"It's a big opportunity," Nadine replied. Her eyes were thoughtful. "The future of people is a powerful thing."

Creating Change at the Local Level

As Nadine and Dan discovered, being able to create the future of your local community is a tremendous opportunity. The work touches countless lives, including those of the people you are closest to, such as family, friends, and loved ones. For me personally, some of the most gratifying experiences in my life have involved working with my local community.

So what's the best way to get involved? There are three pathways I recommend people consider:

- **Become a volunteer.** There's not a community in the world that couldn't use more people donating their time and energy. Look for an organization whose mission you support and believe in. Treat it like a job, listing your skills and seeing where they might be applicable. For example, if you have carpentry skills or experience in project management, you might find an organization committed to the creation of affordable housing in the community. If your background is development, you might get involved with raising money for the local library or community center.

- **Join a cause.** Activism is a great way to engage with like-minded members of the community. Obviously, you should choose an issue you're passionate about, whether it's climate change or education. Activism and volunteerism often go hand in hand, though joining a cause might be less of a time commitment if you're worried about overextending.

- **Run for office.** This approach demands the most skin in the game, but your ability to effect true change in the community will be that much greater. The first step is figuring out which office you want to run for. There are positions at the state, county, and city levels. All the rules of futurecasting apply. Once you've written the story of your future (that is, picked the office you want to run for), you need to find the people, tools, and experts to propel you forward. For example, the website Run for Office enables users to search through more than 150,000 elected offices throughout the US. The League of Women Voters, meanwhile, is committed to helping women get involved in the election process. These types of resources will be invaluable as you put together your backcast.

Up Next: Tech Talk

The future is local, whether you're looking for your next job, the love of your life, or a better tomorrow for your local community. As I've talked about throughout the book, the future is also built by people. There's one final common denominator to futurecasting that I want to share with you, and it's one that strikes fear in many people's hearts. That's right, it's time to talk about technology. But let me assure you, this tech talk, unlike others you've experienced in your life, won't leave you confused and uneasy. Just the opposite. I'm going to show you how you can have control over technology, and how that control is one of the greatest tools in creating the future you desire.

CHAPTER 6

Technology Doesn't Get to Decide the Future, You Do

When people learn that I'm a futurist, technology is always one of the topics they want to talk about first. And why not? Technology, which I'll define as "the application of scientific knowledge for practical use," has been a main driver of human discovery and development ever since some enterprising cave dweller decided to turn a jagged stone into a pickaxe. In my futurecasting process, it's perhaps the single most powerful enabler in the creation of new futures. In short, technology helps make the future possible.

Unfortunately, at some point along the way, the power of technology started to outstrip our basic understanding of it.

Instead of technology being seen as a force for positive change, it became an agent of fear and trepidation. This fact was hammered home to me one evening in 2007, during an audience Q&A session that changed my life forever, and specifically the way I think about the relationship between humans and technology.

The Technophobe in the Crowd

I was standing in front of an audience of about six hundred in a vast event space at the Mark Hopkins Hotel, which sits atop Nob Hill in the heart of San Francisco. The bottom hadn't yet fallen out of the economy, though the first jitters were starting to be felt. I'd been with Intel for about five years at that point and had done enough public speaking that crowds of six hundred or more no longer fazed me. Still, there was a bit of tension in the air as I reached the "Ask me anything" portion of my presentation.

The first few questions ping-ponged from topic to topic. There was a lot of interest in self-driving cars, which were starting to seem a little less like science fiction; earlier that year a team from Carnegie Mellon University had won the Defense Advanced Research Projects Agency (DARPA) autonomous Grand Challenge for self-driven vehicles to navigate through urban streets.

Automation was another hot topic, with several questions riffing on the notion of robots rising up and taking over humanity. After about forty-five minutes, I was ready to wrap things up, so I called for one final question. A man at the back of the room stood up aggressively. He was dressed like your average suburban dad, but something in his manner was off. Even the security guard at the front of the hall seemed to take notice. The man stared coldly toward the stage as an audience runner made his way to him with a microphone.

"Can you answer a question honestly?" the man said, grabbing hold of the microphone, his voice coiled in anger.

"Well, sure." I chuckled, trying to lighten the mood. "I'll do my best."

"Do you really, honestly believe technology has had a positive impact on humanity?" he said. Talk about a loaded question.

"I do." I nodded, as evenly as possible. "I'm a declared optimist. I think that we should use technology to make people's lives better."

"But are we?" he said, his agitated voice causing a screech of distortion in the auditorium speakers. "Are we really? Do you really think technology is making the world a better place?"

The security guard started to move in the direction of the man. The situation was escalating quickly, though I still hadn't quite figured out what was upsetting him so much.

"I certainly think technology *should* make people's lives better," I said. "As a futurist, that's always been the bar I use for success. Are we using technology to make people happier or healthier or at least more productive."

As I spoke, the man nodded vehemently. I couldn't tell if he was agreeing with me or if my words were confirming the very thing that was enraging him.

The security guard reached his row and the man held up his hands.

"It's okay," I said quickly. "Let him finish his question."

The man took a sharp breath and pulled a first-generation iPhone out of his pocket. "Are these things not evil? Don't you see the harm they're doing to our children? My daughters can't even carry on a conversation anymore. How are they going to get jobs? What are their futures going to be like? Can you tell me that?"

I finally understood the man's question, or maybe it's more accurate to say I understood the question behind the question. He felt that technology was harming his daughters and robbing them of their future. In his mind at that moment I, as a futurist, was responsible for stealing his daughters' future, for stealing his daughters from him.

"So you think that this technology is harming you daughters?" I asked.

"I do," he said, nodding sharply.

The packed audience was on the edge of their seats. Their heads moved back and forth from my position on the stage to the back of the room and the angry man with the phone. They weren't sure if they should get out of there quickly or hang back to hear my answer.

"Good," I said loudly, leaning into the microphone.

This caught the man off guard. Actually it caught the whole room off guard. Was I really about to validate his anger?

"Good," I repeated after a pause. "You are upset because you believe that this technology is harming your family. We need more of that. We need more parents who are passionate about their children's welfare and future."

The man relaxed, the tension melting from his shoulders. The arm that was holding the phone high in the air slowly fell to his side. He didn't know what to say or how to reply.

"But let's talk about this technology," I continued. "Smartphones are still pretty new, and I would say that we don't know yet what's good or bad about them. We don't know what's socially acceptable. But the thing we always have to remember is that we are in charge. We get to decide what we do with any new technology."

The man might have been less distraught, but he wasn't buying what I was saying.

"Okay, I can see you don't believe me," I pushed further. "Let me give you a specific example of what I'm talking about. Are you a family that watches TV during dinner?"

"No, we never have the TV on during dinner," the man answered.

"Okay, great!" I said, allowing myself to get a little more excited. The audience was also getting back to normal. "That's a decision you get to make as a father and as a family. You're in control. The TV doesn't get to decide."

"I guess I see what you mean," the man replied, somewhat lost in thought as he continued to process what I was saying.

I was eager to give more examples of how technology existed as a tool of the people, for example the use of video games in the treatment of mental illness or how new financial instruments were easing the burden of poverty. In fact, the very smartphone the man was holding in his hand, with so much consternation, was at that moment being used by the US military to help in the management and treatment of post-traumatic stress disorder, or PTSD. Doctors, therapists, and even family members can't be with afflicted soldiers at all times, but a smartphone can. Instead of seeing this technology as driving a wedge between people and the real world, we can see it as a proxy, taking care of the people we love, keeping watch over them, and reaching out when they're in their darkest hours. In this way technology helps people heal, a point I could have made over and over again to the man in the crowd. But another voice broke out over the auditorium sound system.

"Okay, great, thank you everyone," it said. This was Brenda, my host for the evening talk. As she climbed up the short flight of stairs onto the stage, she continued, "And thank you, BDJ, for the talk and giving so much time for questions. Can we get another round of applause for BDJ?"

The audience clapped and began to gather their things to go.

"Well, *that* was exciting," Brenda said, throwing an arm around my shoulders.

"Yeah." I smiled. "It was a good question at the end there." I scanned the audience for the man, but he had already disappeared into the crowd.

A Twenty-First-Century Fear of Technology

That night in San Francisco changed my worldview and the work I do as a futurist. I realized in that moment that I have an important responsibility to people, which is to help them understand that technology doesn't get to decide the future. They do. *You* do. This belief is another fundamental of futurecasting, along with the ideas that the future is built by people and that all futures are local. The two latter tenets can be a little abstract, making it hard for people to wrap their heads around them, but people usually get there in the end.

The technology point is an even harder sell. That's because people in the twenty-first century have a tremendous amount of fear and anxiety around technology and its impact on their lives.

I meet individuals all the time who, like the man in San Francisco, are terrified that technology is taking away their future and, what's more, that they're powerless to do anything about it. This mindset has become more common in the last couple of decades, as technology itself has become increasingly complicated. People feel like they can't understand it, let alone master it. In fact, according to Chapman University's latest annual Survey of American Fears, based on a sample of fifteen hundred adult Americans, three of the five biggest fears are technology-related: cyberterrorism, corporate tracking of personal information, and government tracking of personal information.

To some extent, this is the will of tech companies, which spend billions of dollars creating increasingly sophisticated technologies that spread around the globe like a virus, disrupting businesses and changing cultures. "It feels like the future is coming faster and faster each day," people tell me time and time again. It's like we're standing before a massive tsunami of technology with the power to wash away the world as we know it. The tech companies don't mind this, since it allows them to control the narrative.

Add children into the mix, and our collective fear borders on hysteria. Like the angry middle-aged man in San Francisco, people don't know how to protect the very thing in their lives they care most about, even more than themselves.

I get it. I understood the man's anger and frustration, and I also understood why he would want to blame me personally.

But here's the thing: it's not true. Technology is not in control of the future, and neither are the companies that develop it. You are. People make the future, not technology. Yes, technology will have a sizable and significant effect on your future. But you are not powerless before it. How do I know this? Because we've been here before.

A Historian and a Futurist Walk into a Bar . . .

People are always surprised when they learn that I work closely with historians. They assume futurists and historians are rival gangs, like the Sharks and the Jets, the Capulets and the Montagues, dogs and cats. As if we are two groups that couldn't possibly get along. Nothing could be further from the truth. History gives us a language and a framework to talk about what's coming next. And if we're going to discuss technology, we need to start by talking about the history of humans and machines.

One of my favorite sparring partners in this debate is James Carrott, a historian and self-described contrarian who very much looks the part, with his towering frame, long red beard, and small circular John Lennon glasses. James explores the intersection between history and culture and how this intersection affects the future.

Back in 2018 I met James for a beer near his home in Seattle.

In addition to his probing intellect, I love the fact that James knows the best places to sample the latest craft beers. For this outing, he took us to the Pike Brewing Company, located in the world-renowned Pike Place Market. The place is jammed with shops and food vendors, including fishmongers famous for hurling the catches of the day through the air to often unsuspecting customers. Order up a fresh Chinook salmon, pulled that morning from the cold waters around Seattle, and they'll clean it right in front of you and then chuck it across the market to the checkout guy, who will wrap it up in newspaper for you to take home.

After taking in the sights and sounds and smells of the market, James and I saddled up to the bar at Pike's and ordered a couple of IPAs.

"The past is the on-ramp to the future," James once told me, early on in our collaboration. "History in fact does not repeat itself. But history is the language we use to talk about the future. We have no other language, no other words to describe what is coming in the future. We always have to compare it to what we have experienced in the past."

I wanted to pick the conversation up with James today in the context of people's fear of technology. Surely this can't be a new thing, I thought. What lessons about technology from the past would leave us better prepared for tomorrow and able to see our future more clearly?

"Anxiety around technology seems to be growing," I started.

"There's a very specific and palpable fear shared by so many people I meet that technology is going to shape their future. Or more specifically, that technology is in control of their future."

"Oh, I totally agree," James said, taking off his glasses and cleaning them absentmindedly, his go-to gesture when he's about to go deep into thought. "Everywhere you turn we're being told that our lives will never be the same again because of some new technology or some new technological revolution. Heck, I live in Seattle. This is practically ground zero for that kind of thinking."

"But this can't be new," I jumped in. "Technology has been around for—"

"A long, long, long time," James said, finishing my thought. "You could start with the hand axe, really."

"Right," I said. "But people didn't have these kinds of feelings about the hand axe. It wasn't a world-changing revolution, it was just a tool that worked."

"Part of the problem is advertising," James replied. "The tech companies want you to believe in revolution. It's more compelling and sexy than hawking a tool that just plain works."

"Agreed," I said. "But you have to admit that today's fear and anxiety around technology is magnitudes greater than anything we've seen before."

"Maybe," James allowed. "But if you want to trace the origins of that anxiety, it goes back to the technological advances during the world wars of the last century, culminating in the nuclear bombs that decimated Hiroshima and Nagasaki. That changed everything."

"How come exactly?" I asked.

"The scale was just so big," James replied. "It's one thing to shoot a person with a gun, but it's a whole other thing to press a button and decimate entire cities. The scale of the thing was way too big for people to wrap their heads around it."

"And the scale of technology continues to scare people today?" I asked.

"In the middle of the twentieth century people looked to the wonders of science," James continued. He put his hands in front of my face and wiggled his fingers like he was doing magic. "People imagined impossible futures where science solved all our problems and changed everything. It held great promise in the beginning. But as the scale of the technology increased, it began to overwhelm. Take nuclear fission, for example. Who really understands it? These concepts are so big, their scale is so huge, that we can't understand them, and so we don't feel that we have power over them. They have power over us."

As James spoke, my mind went to a man named Dr. Keith Devlin, also known as the Math Guy. He's the executive director of Stanford University's Human Sciences and Technologies Advanced Research Institute, and he has a bunch of other titles as well. But mostly Keith just loves teaching math and getting people to think differently about it.

His belief is that most of us don't know what math really is. As he explained once, "Math isn't about computation and calculation and solving equations. It's about thinking about the world in a certain way that we have learned over the centuries is extremely powerful."[*]

Keith calls this "mathematical thinking," and I think it's helpful for us when we consider the future of technology, especially in light of my conversation with James. "Mathematics exists as a psychological and a social construct," Keith says. "When you're doing mathematics, what you're doing is learning more about the world. What you're really learning about is how the human mind encounters and makes sense of the world. It's really a mirror. So mathematics in some sense is a lens through which you look at the world. But in a deeper sense, it's a mirror through which you look at yourself in a very abstract and penetrating way."

I shared this perspective with James, then added, "We can think about technology in the same way. It's simply a tool to help us look at the world and our place in it. We need to remember that we're the ones at the center, and that technology ultimately is a way for us to better understand ourselves, our fellow humans, and our futures."

"That will certainly help reduce the scale of technology to a more manageable size," he said. "And give us back some power over the destiny of our lives. It's the Magna Carta all over again."

---

[*] Keith Devlin, "The Joy of Math: Learning and What it Means To Be Human," interview by Krista Tippett, *On Being*, NPR, September 19, 2013," https://onbeing.org /programs/keith-devlin-the-joy-of-math-learning-and-what-it-means-to-be-human/.

"The what?" I asked.

"You know, the 1215 treaty," he said, shooting me his best *Duh* face. "All of this ultimately goes back to the Renaissance."

"Hold that thought!" I shouted. I could see James was about to get even deeper. "Let me get us another round. Then you can tell me all about the birth of scientific thought."

LET'S TALK TECH
Quick Questions 5

Okay, history lesson complete, let's hit the pause button here and figure out more of your thoughts and feelings on technology. The quick bit of level setting will be helpful as we dig deeper into the discussion. Obviously everyone's relationship to technology is unique, shaped largely by their upbringing and early childhood experiences.

In my case, my father was an electrical engineer and my mother was an IT specialist. This was the 1970s. Mom used to bring home these crazy things called PCs, or personal computers, for me to tinker with on the weekend. I also recall Dad bringing home electrical schematics from the radar lab, unrolling the large pieces of paper on the kitchen table. He'd trace the path of the electricity and explain how the various components worked. It was like a story for me. A few weeks later he'd bring home the decommissioned part and let me take it apart, physically exploring the story he'd told me earlier. You might almost say I was raised to be a futurist. At the very least, my folks instilled in me a fascination for technology, for which I'm eternally grateful.

What about you? What's your view on technology? To unpack that question, I want you to write your answers to the following questions in your journal.

QUESTION 1

What is an experience from your childhood in which technology played a big role?

This is to get you thinking about your past relationship to technology. I once asked this question of a friend, and he told a harrowing tale of taking apart a remote-control car to try to figure out how it worked only to be scolded by his dad for wasting money. Poor kid spent weeks trying to put the car back together. He's on the more tech-averse side of the spectrum.

For others, technology unlocked a world of wonder and imagination. From video games to robots, kids are often in love with technology. I build robots with kids, and they come up with the most amazing ideas. I've seen robots that wear capes or overalls, a robot that has a switch on the back of its head to tell either GOOD or BAD jokes. I have even built a robot that farts. You should see the pure joy that explodes from both young and more mature people when a robot stops doing a task and lets out a fart. For many, technology can be full of wonder and humor.

Let's see where you are.

FOLLOW-UP QUESTIONS:

- **How did that experience (from Question 1) shape your worldview of technology?**

- **Did it make you want different things from not only technology but also the world in general?**

- **What do you wish your experience with technology had been when you were young?**

When I talk to people, they are often split into two groups: those who wish they'd had more tech in their childhood and those who wish they'd had less. It can be helpful to talk about not only what you experienced but also now, later in life, what you wish had happened.

QUESTION 2

What are three positive and three negative things about smartphones?

This part of the exercise is intended to capture your current feelings about technology. For most people, it's not an either-or decision. There are things you like about smartphones and things you don't like. Let's get a better handle on where you fall today.

FOLLOW-UP QUESTIONS:

- **Who do you blame or credit for the negatives or positives?**

- **How has your relationship with your phone changed over the years?**

- **When you speak about your phone with your friends, parents, or kids, how do you refer to it?**

We all have a complex relationship with technology. It has become an integral part of our lives. But this is nothing new. Fifty-six percent of Americans name their cars. We humanize our technologies because they are such a big part of our daily routines. The more complex the technology, the more complex the relationship.

QUESTION 3

What is the impact automation could have on your profession in the next ten years?

Now we're looking out into the future. There's no shortage of doomsday scenarios around robots, job loss, and the like. Without influencing your answer too much, I tend to think those fears are overblown. But what are your thoughts? Certainly answers will vary depending on the type of work you do. Are there other factors that contribute to your thinking?

FOLLOW-UP QUESTIONS:

- **What is the future you want to have with technology?**

- **Is there any way your relationship with technology could be better?**

- **Who do you think has control?**

These follow-up questions get to the meat of why people have such anxiety over technology. It's about control. I'll hold off any further armchair analysis at this time, except to reiterate the point that your relationship to technology was shaped by forces beyond your control. But the same is true of everything else. The difference with technology is that it plays such an outsize role in our culture and so its mystery can feel a little terrifying. I hope by getting you to think more deeply about your relationship with technology, maybe for the first time ever, you see that you're actually the one in control.

Technology as Just Another Tool

When we think about technology and its effect on our future, we need to understand that any feelings of fear are not of the technology itself but rather of our own feelings of powerlessness. It's a fear of a complexity that we might never understand.

The technology itself doesn't have any power. Technology is just a tool. Tools in and of themselves are useless and not very interesting. A hammer is just a hammer. It only becomes interesting and relevant when you use it to build stuff—a boat, a house, a wagon for your kid to ride around in. Tools are only meaningful when they have an impact on people's lives.

Like I told the audience in San Francisco, we need to judge the worthiness of any technology by how it touches people's lives. How are we using this technology to make people's lives better? More specifically, how can you use technology to make your life better? How will you use technology as a tool to help you realize the future you want and avoid the future you don't want?

If we change the way we think about technology, if we can remember that its power is in the hands of humans, we take the first step toward a different future. Once we see ourselves in a new future, we can look to technology as simply a tool, an enabler to propel us toward that future.

The power of technology to make people's lives better is the cornerstone of all the work I do as a futurist. I'm forever looking for ways to put humans at the center. This is not simply a theory. It's something I put into practice. I always judge technology with this bar in mind. Usually the best place to do this is with the most vulnerable people: children and the elderly. If a technology can make them healthier, happier, and more secure, then it's got a good chance of succeeding. Let me show you what I mean.

Surrounded by Giants

"I saw another cadet go into the fountain before we left," Al said suddenly, breaking a long stretch of silence.

Al was short for Alfredo. "Like the pasta sauce," as he likes to say the first time he meets someone. I'd been working with Al long enough that the joke had moved from funny to corny to finally a little weird if he didn't say it.

"You saw what?" I asked. I was riding shotgun next to Al as we headed north on Highway 25 from Colorado Springs to Denver. It was late afternoon and I was resting my eyes after a long day.

"Sorry, BDJ, were you sleeping?" Al asked. "I was just saying that I saw another cadet throw themselves into the fountain at the academy when I was on my way to meet you."

"Oh, that," I said. "Yes, it's that time of year. I think I saw three of them on this trip."

Al and I were doing some threatcasting work with the US Air Force Academy, or USAFA, as everyone calls it. Al is a security researcher based out of Denver. He was giving me a ride north so I could catch a flight back home to Oregon the next morning.

Now to the fountain. At the end of the academic year, it's a tradition with senior cadets to throw themselves into the Air Garden fountain, usually in full military garb, after their final exam. Their joy is infectious.

The car went silent again and I closed my eyes, the engine noise almost lulling me back to sleep.

Al shifted in the driver's seat, causing the entire car to rock. He's a big guy, both vertically and horizontally. He spent most of his life in the Secret Service and now does security research for high-tech companies and the military.

"Everything okay, big fella?" I asked without opening my eyes.

"Yeah," he said. "I mean no, but yeah."

"What's up?" I asked. "Do you need me to drive?"

"I think I do actually," he replied sheepishly. "I'm not sleeping much these days."

"No problem at all." I perked up. "I'm glad you said something."

We pulled over, switched seats, and got back on the road. The landscapes between Colorado Springs and Denver are breathtaking, with monumental ridges and mountaintops that looked ancient in the golden afternoon light.

"You're not sleeping?" I asked. "Everything okay?"

"I don't think I've slept more than two hours straight since the boys were diagnosed," Al said, referring to his sons, aged nine and twelve. They had been diagnosed with type 1 diabetes within a few months of each other about five years earlier. He went on: "The high and low blood sugars that happen in the middle of the night are part of it, but my wife and I have it pretty much under control. Lately, it's the worry that's keeping me up at night. I'm worried about their future. Any thoughts?"

"Gosh," I exhaled. "I've never done any work on the future of diabetes."

"It's funny, everyone always tells you a cure is five years out," Al went on. "I met a guy the other day who has lived with diabetes for thirty years. When I mentioned the five-year promise, he laughed and said that's exactly the timeline he was given when he was first diagnosed."

"Ugh," I said, shaking my head.

"Yeah, not a lot of hope there," Al said, rapping the dashboard with his thick fingers. "But that's not what I was asking you. I know you don't work in diabetes. What I really want to talk about is technology. What technology is coming down the pike that could help my kids? I'd love to be able to futurecast that."

"Well," I said, glancing down at my watch, "it's still an hour to Denver. Let's dig into it."

Outside, the light was starting to fade. The mountains were silhouettes of giants on the horizon.

"I typically start by asking people, 'What's the future you want and what's the future you want to avoid?' But I think you already know that, right?"

"Yes." Al nodded. "If there is no cure, I want my boys to be as healthy as they can be. That means getting them the best and latest technology to manage their condition."

"How has the technology helped so far?" I asked.

"It's been a savior," Al said flatly. "They have their CGM."

"CGM?"

"Continuous glucose monitor," he explained. "It tracks their blood sugar in real time and sends the info right to my phone." He held up his phone with the app open.

"Wow," I said.

"Then there's the pump that delivers insulin exactly calibrated to the CGM."

"That's great."

"It is great," he replied, running the backs of his fingers along his mustache. "The only trouble is, I'm not sure what other technology I'm missing or what new things are in the works."

"FOMO," I said, referring to "fear of missing out," an all-too-common condition of the modern technological age. It often applies to teenagers on social media, but we all experience FOMO at times, including around the health and wellness of our children.

"Yeah," Al agreed. "It all feels so beyond my control, like I'm at the mercy of doctors and insurance providers and big faceless biotech companies."

"I think that's the future we're talking about," I said. "It's the one in which you *are* doing the most you can, without the fear that you're leaving some critical box unchecked."

He shook his head. "I don't understand."

"You want a future in which you are doing everything that you can possibly do and at the same time you feel assured that you've got all the bases covered, that there's not more to be done. A future in which you've conquered all the unknown unknowns."

"Maybe," he said, still not entirely clear.

"There are two parts to the future you want. The first is doing everything you can; the second is knowing you're taking all the available steps. The hard part about unknown unknowns is precisely that they're unknown. What people need is assurance, and the feeling of being in control."

"That's it!" Al bellowed. "I don't feel in control. There are all these big companies out there spending millions of dollars. How can I make them part of our future?"

"Let's break it down," I said. "Let's use the process."

The sky was now pitch-black. If we hadn't seen the landscape at dusk, we never would've known we were surrounded by giants.

"We know the future you want," I started. "You want to make sure that you're doing all you can and feel like you have control over the process. Now we need to figure out who the people are who can help you do that."

"Well, there are our doctors and the rest of the medical team," Al answered.

"But who else?" I pushed. "Remember, we want to go further out."

"You mean like researchers and biotech companies?"

"Yes," I said. "You need to write down who is doing work in

that area. What universities? What companies? Are there support groups or people sharing the research? If you start looking and asking, you will get a well-rounded idea of what is actually going on."

Al took out a pen and pad and started to jot down ideas. There was his local chapter of the Juvenile Diabetes Research Foundation, which he'd been slow to get involved with. And the Diabetes Research Institute Foundation in Florida, the only group in the world 100 percent committed to discovering a biological cure for the disease.

"The DRI is doing some amazing work around cell transplants," Al said. "But I don't really understand it all."

"You need to change that," I said.

We then moved into the role of tools in the futurecasting process. "These are technologies or organizations that will help to propel you toward the future you want," I said.

Al brainstormed more ideas. He would need to do a lot more research, but he was surprised by how much knowledge and information he had absorbed by living with the disease for five years. He had just never taken the time to gather it all in one place. I see this all the time in futurecasting. Once people give themselves the permission and mental space to think about their future, the parts start to fall into place. More work is always needed, but allowing yourself to imagine the future is such a critical phase of the journey.

"Finally, there are the experts," I told Al. "Who are the people who have done this before? Who has successfully realized the future you envision?"

"It's funny you ask that," Al began. "There's this company in California called Bigfoot Biomedical that's doing a lot of revolutionary work around insulin delivery. It was started by this whiz kid in quantitative finance whose young son was diagnosed with T1D. He quit his job and made it his mission to make life easier for diabetics and their families. I've wanted to reach out to them, but I just haven't found the time."

The lights of the Denver cityscape sparkled in the distance. We were almost out of road, but I wanted to leave Al with his marching orders. I launched into the backcast.

If the future was a place where Al had full control of the technology available for the treatment and potential cure of his kids' diabetes, his halfway point might include an active involvement in Bigfoot, the Diabetes Research Institute Foundation, and any other groups his research turned up. Partway would involve reaching out to these groups through any personal connections he was able to identify. Monday would be a continuation of the process we had started on Highway 25, brainstorming ideas and making a comprehensive to-do list.

"You know, BDJ," Al said as we exited into Denver International Airport, "I haven't felt this good about the future in five years. I think I might actually get some sleep tonight. At least until one of the boys goes low at 3 a.m."

"Glad to hear it, Al," I said. "And based on what you've told me about technology and diabetes treatment, those overnight lows could soon be a thing of the past as well."

Future-Proofing Your Profession

Through the futurecasting process, Alfredo turned his fear of technology into one of his family's most valuable assets. Whereas he once felt at the mercy of technology, he's now the one in charge. His boys continue to thrive, and he is even exploring several exciting clinical trials.

Al's fear of technology actually had nothing to do with technology at all. It was about power and complexity. As James, my historian friend, explained, when the scale gets too big, people turn to fear. They worry they will never understand the technology and it will shape their lives in ways they can't control.

As with the angry audience member in San Francisco, Al's fear and the passion that fueled it were heightened by his love and devotion for his children. He knew the future he wanted and also the future he wanted to avoid. He just didn't know how to get there. Fear clouded his vision.

As we know, the future is built by people and it's local. The people building the future are regular individuals who live and work somewhere. They are building future technologies in a specific place, alongside other people. They can be found, as Al's story shows.

This is the relationship to technology that I want everyone to have. Technology is here to serve people. It's a tool. For every client I've helped, from large multinationals to the random guy sitting next to me on the airplane, technology was one of the tools that would help propel them toward their desired future in every case.

Of course there is such a thing as technology overload. I take a week every summer climbing up the backside of Mount Hood, to a campsite with no electricity, running water, or cell service, thanks to the towering trees of the Pacific Northwest. It's my annual detox. But the rest of the time, technology is an inevitability.

Nowhere is this more apparent than the workplace. I now want to turn our attention to it, specifically to the fear of workplace automation. When it comes to technology, this is the fear that people express to me most often. They worry that technology in some form—robots, computers, machines—is going to render their profession obsolete. It's the fear that keeps them up at night more than any other.

The Machines Are Going to Take Your Job
(Well . . . Kind Of)

When people come to me with this doomsday scenario, my usual answer is that if a robot can take your job, your job probably sucked. Tough love, I know, but it's true. If a machine can truly replace you, that means your job was turning you into a machine.

You're not a machine. You're a human being. So your job was not valuing your humanity or who you are as a person.

Still, while it's true that if a machine takes your job it means your job probably sucked, I realize that your paycheck didn't suck at all. That's the real fear here. People worry they will be replaced by technology and left with nowhere to work. According to a 2018 study out of Baylor University, by sociologist and researcher Paul K. McClure, technophobes are more likely than non-technophobes to suffer anxiety-related mental health issues and to fear job loss and financial insecurity. Advances in robotics and artificial intelligence are exacerbating those concerns among a substantial portion of the US population at an alarming rate.

And why not? It's true that more and more human tasks are being automated. But it's critical to remember that it's not technology that's replacing you. It's the people who run organizations and companies. And you can keep an eye on them. They will indicate what they're doing, where they're investing, and how they might save on labor costs by using technology to replace workers. This is a real thing. But it's also not a new thing. Again, we've been here before.

Averting the Apocalypse

If history is the language we use to talk about the future, then maybe James could help us understand how to deal with this possible future. It sure is nice having a historian on speed dial. I called him up.

"As you know, I'm an optimist about the future," I started.

"Yes, I remember," James said, clearing his throat ahead of a good long chat.

"And yet there are so many forces out there that scare the crap out of people and make them pessimistic about the future," I said. "Top of the list: the fear of workplace automation."

"The robot apocalypse!" James cried.

"That might be a little extreme," I said. "But yes, it's the fear of technological unemployment."

"Well, that's inevitable," James replied flatly. "As long as we've had technology, it's been replacing the work of humans. That's what humans do. We invent technology and machines to do our work for us. We're really, really good at it."

"But as we look out into the future, the impact could be pretty big," I said.

"History is littered with examples of machines replacing human labor, with massive economic and social consequences. Think back to legendary Ned Ludd, supposedly smashing looms in eighteenth-century England after he lost his job to the newfangled machines."

"That's where we get the term 'Luddite,'" I said.

"That's right. Today, if people are against technology they're called a Luddite, in homage to Ned Ludd and the general resistance to machine automation. John Henry is another example, from American folklore. 'John Henry was a steel driving man,'" James sang in a mock baritone, borrowing from the old folk song.

Being an American schoolkid I knew the story well, the steel driver who vanquished the steam-powered machine but paid for the victory with his life.

"That's really a dark story to tell schoolkids," I reflected.

"True, but it's a good lesson," James replied.

"So what do we do about it?" I asked. "If workplace automation has such a long history, with no sign of letting up in the future, is there a way to think about it to remove some of the fear?"

"For starters, people need to understand that automation is about scale. It allows companies to not only reduce labor costs but also take productivity to scale. Machines work fast, they never get tired, and they can be optimized in ways that humans can't."

"This applies to all tech," I added. "Both to physical machines and digital technology. Factories, self-driving cars, artificial intelligence."

"Or even the internet," James agreed. "Lots of people lost their jobs to the internet. Like travel agents—there aren't many of those anymore. When jobs get automated, they can then be scaled up, the businesses get big, and that's the thing—because they're big they have a big impact on culture and economics, but they are also highly visible. People see what's happening, they see jobs going away, and they start to worry."

"So as we think about the future, what should we consider?" I asked.

"Well, for starters, the fact that all the jobs won't go away,"

James answered. "For all the headlines about home automation, guess how many jobs have become entirely obsolete?"

"I give up," I said. "How many?"

"One," James answered. "Of the 270 occupations listed in the 1950 census by the Bureau of Labor Statistics, exactly one no longer exists. Care to guess what it is?"

"Enlighten me," I said.

"Elevator operator," James said. "It's the only job that's actually disappeared. The truth is, there are still plenty of jobs to choose from, and there always will be. Specialty jobs, trades, crafts, and anything that's human, like taking care of people or talking with people. People like people, and there are some jobs that we simply don't want machines to do for us."

"Like being human?" I said, recalling another line from Dr. Keith Devlin, that we should spend more time letting the brain do things that the brain is really well suited for that computers can't do very well: making value judgments, making analogical leaps.

"That and keeping us out of a nuclear war," James said.

"Nuclear war?" I said.

"During the Cold War, when the US and the Soviet Union were poised to nuke each other to smithereens, there was a soldier in the Soviet Air Defense Forces named Stanislav Petrov. In 1983, he was on duty at the Soviet nuclear early warning command center. It was a tense time. A few weeks earlier the Soviets had shot down a Korean airliner. All of a sudden the system goes nuts and starts telling Petrov that the US has launched nuclear missiles at

Russia. The machines were basically saying that World War III had just started."

"Global nuclear war," I added.

"Yeah, everyone's worst fear," James continued. "And Petrov was watching the first strike. Here's the thing, though: Petrov didn't launch a counterstrike. All his training, Soviet military protocol, everything was telling him to launch a counterattack, but he didn't do it. And why not? Because he knew there was no way the US would attack, knowing full well that the Soviets would launch a counterattack and everyone would die. He judged it to be a false alarm, a system malfunction, which is exactly what it was. He disobeyed orders and saved the world."

"Wow, that's some story," I said.

"It's also a great example of why some jobs should never be given over to the machines," James said. "If Stanislav Petrov's job had been automated, there's a very good chance we wouldn't be here today."

Defending Against Job Automation

Humans get to decide the future, not technology. Nevertheless, there are instances of machines replacing specific human tasks, and that trend likely won't slow down. Some of the early scientific papers portended a particularly gloomy future.

In 2013, for example, two University of Oxford researchers, Carl Benedikt Frey and Michael A. Osborne, released a report called *The Future of Employment: How Susceptible Are Jobs to Computerization?* They concluded that over the next twenty years, nearly 50 percent of all jobs could disappear completely. In 2015, another report, by the Organisation for Economic Co-operation and Development, was slightly less pessimistic, finding 14 percent of jobs to be "highly vulnerable." Then came a correction to this dystopian view as new research revealed that automation actually created more jobs in the economy than it destroyed.

The truth, in my opinion, is probably somewhere in the middle. Automation will benefit the job market in certain areas while creating stress and disruption in others. Likewise, the impact of technology on different professions won't always be black and white, with winners on one side and losers on the other. I was reminded of this during a recent visit to New York City, where I was giving a guest lecture to students at New York University.

After the lecture, Kim, the hosting professor, asked if I would come around to meet her family. "You have to talk some sense into my daughter, Alex," she said as we walked from campus to the subway station. "She's studying to be a CPA."

"Really?" I asked. "Does she know that CPA jobs are going away?"

"I told her that. But she says she really loves numbers and insists it will be a good career."

When we arrived at Kim's apartment, I met her wife, Georgina, and their daughter, Alex. After introductions were taken care of, I sat down with Alex to have a chat.

"Your mom tells me you want to be a CPA," I said.

"That's right!" She smiled. "She probably told you to talk some sense into me."

"That she did." I nodded. "As a futurist, I need to tell you that because of automation and artificial intelligence, accountants are going the way of milkmen and switchboard operators."

"Yeah, I know," she said. "That's why I'm also getting a minor in systems engineering."

"Come again?" I said.

"I'm going to be the one to help integrate all that artificial intelligence into the accounting. I'm going to be the CPA that makes other CPAs obsolete."

"Wow," I said. She was right. Financial firms are going to need to hire CPAs to train the artificial intelligence. Alex had successfully futurecasted her own career.

"I'm a numbers person," she added. "I've always wanted to be a CPA."

She didn't need my help at all. "Have you ever thought about a career as a futurist?" I asked as we made our way back to dinner.

As Alex's story demonstrates, even professions that are highly vulnerable to automation, like accounting, can be future-proofed. Alex's strategy is one I often advocate: embracing innovation. On the face of it, AI poses an existential threat to accountants. Alex turned that thinking on its head and made AI a tool in her career building.

There are other strategies you should deploy in your defense against professional obsolescence. For starters, it's vital to be in a continuous state of learning. Information is constantly evolving. I don't care if you just graduated from Harvard; you're already behind on some of the latest developments in your field. That's why you need to treat education as a lifetime commitment. That doesn't mean you have to be enrolled in coursework full-time (though occasionally getting back into a classroom does wonders for the mind). You can also read a book related to your work. Or join a professional network. The important thing is to actively stay engaged in your rapidly evolving industry.

You also need to expand your skill set at all times. A diverse skill set has always been valuable in the workplace, and it will become even more so as automation increases. Focus on behavioral skills, since human-based tasks will be the least vulnerable to automation. If you're lacking in communication skills, including reading and writing, find a workshop or peer group devoted to them. If you lack leadership skills, like motivating team members and resolving conflicts, find ways to develop them, maybe through volunteer work.

Lastly, remember to stay human. It bears repeating that people are at the center of everything we do as humans. No matter how advanced machine learning gets, no matter how sophisticated AI becomes, nothing can replace human-to-human interaction. The more emotional intelligence you bring to your work, the more indispensable you will be. Qualities like humor, empathy, and mentalization, or the ability to understand the mental state that underlies a person's overt behavior, will become even more valuable in the future. I realize that not everyone is a people person. But even the deepest of introverts can find ways to form new human connections within the workplace—to the great benefit of their longtime employability.

Up Next: The Mother of All Fears

Technology is at the root of so many future fears. As you now know from reading this chapter, that fear is unfounded. By taking the power back from technology, you take away the fear. I wish that was the final word on fear in the futurecasting process. Unfortunately, there is still much, much more to say on the topic. "The only thing we have to fear is fear itself," FDR famously said. True, perhaps. But getting to the heart of that fear is no easy feat. It is, however, entirely doable. As with everything in futurecasting, the first step is to get started.

CHAPTER 7

All Our Dark Places

I want to switch things up here and start this chapter with a Quick Questions exercise. This one is designed to take on fear—the big fears in our lives.

Way back in chapter 2 we talked about the fear of the unknown as it relates to the future. This kind of fear can rule your life, holding you back from the future you desire and deserve. We faced that fear together, head-on, showing how you have the power to shape your own future. With the help of people, places, and technology, you discovered how you can not only imagine your future but get there as well. You don't need to be paralyzed by fear. You can overcome it.

I believe that with every fiber of my being. But I also know that all fears are not created equal. Some fears are not at all simple or straightforward. Some fears wake us up in the middle of the night, assuming they let us go to sleep at all. These are the big fears, the existential fears that overwhelm us and leave us powerless. Their darkness is harder to overcome, but we can use the same process to find a ray of hope, to give us something to believe in and build upon.

STARING DOWN FEAR
Quick Questions 6

Okay, let's get journaling by answering the following three questions.

QUESTION 1
What's the most scared you've ever been in your life?

We have all lived through some incredibly harrowing global events, from 9/11 to COVID-19. Maybe it was during them that you experienced the highest level of fear. Or if you or a loved one has ever received a serious health diagnosis, it no doubt sparked a tremendous amount of fear. Or maybe it was an early childhood experience, being separated from your parent in a crowded space or having a close encounter with a stray animal. Once you settle on the moment of super-heightened fear, describe some of the feelings around it. Fear will certainly be at the core, but what else do you remember feeling? Anger, confusion, powerlessness, guilt? Do your best to capture your specific frame of mind at that moment in time.

FOLLOW-UP QUESTIONS:

- **What are your feelings today about the same experience?**

- **How do you think you will feel about this experience ten years from now?**

Take a moment to think about how your feelings have evolved since the original event. How has the fear shifted shape? Maybe it's mellowed over time or maybe it's intensified, the way an untreated injury or ailment gets worse over time. Just as with the first question, try to isolate any specific feelings or emotions associated with this memory. The more specific you can be with the exercise, the better.

You thought about now versus then. Next I want you to think about now versus tomorrow. How much control do you think you have over this seminal life experience? Will it follow the same trajectory? Or do you think it will take on a different dimension over time?

QUESTION 2

What keeps you up at night?

Our fears change throughout our lives. What scares us as kids is different from the anxiety we have as young adults making our way into the world. The concerns of a parent can be shaped differently than the worries we have as we move into our golden years. But we are talking about the big fears, the ones you don't think you would talk about in polite conversation.

FOLLOW-UP QUESTIONS:

- **How does this fear shape your life today?**

- **Do you take precautions?**

- **Have you ever talked to anyone about it? What did you say?**

Much of our lives are ruled by fear, anxiety, and worry. These emotions rob us of our future. They make us brittle. Recognizing your fears and the deep power they might have over your actions can help you to do something about them.

QUESTION 3

What's the worst thing that could happen in the future?

This is an important question we will come back to later in this chapter. The worst-case scenario is a powerful tool as we think about the future, but it is a way of thinking that is taboo for many people. They don't want to think about the really dark places. Some might think it's morbid to even have these thoughts, but it's not unhealthy if you're going to put these visions to use to make your life better.

FOLLOW-UP QUESTIONS:

- Do you feel like you have any control at all over this?

- What is an indicator that this dark future is starting to happen?

This is how you start to take power away from the darker fears. Finding what you have control over is a first step, even if that control is small. (We'll explore this too later in the chapter.) In typical backcasting form, understanding the details around what it will take for this future to happen is important. Going to these dark places and coming back can help us all build a brighter tomorrow.

Real Dark, Real Fast

One of my claims to fame as a futurist is inventing the process called threatcasting, which you may recall from chapter 3. It is as it sounds: identifying future threats and coming up with strategies for dealing with them. The threats could be aimed at businesses but also at national security or economic stability. My team and I first identify possible threats, then figure out how best to disrupt, mitigate, and recover from them.

I've used threatcasting with the US Army, the Federal Emergency Management Agency (FEMA), and a wide range of private companies. We've explored the future of nuclear proliferation, the weaponization of artificial intelligence, and what it would mean to experience a digital weapon of mass destruction. The work is not for the faint of heart. But it is empowering. In the Threatcasting Lab at Arizona State University that I run, our motto is "Envisioning futures to empower action." That's really our goal. Not just to come up with possible dark futures but to provide concrete steps that can be taken to avoid them.

At the lab, we also have an unofficial motto: "Real dark, real fast." Because our job is to get to these threats as quickly as possible so that we can begin the work of making them better. Real dark, real fast is also what happens at parties and barbecues when people ask me what I'm working on. I start talking, sometimes forgetting that, for most people, exploring widespread use of biological weapons is not a typical Wednesday. So I often see that look on people's faces when I've gotten a little too dark a little too fast. They get uncomfortable, shuffle their feet, and start staring at their hotdog. Yep, I'm that guy at the party. Fortunately, I'm usually able to recognize it, and I'll quickly turn the conversation back to baseball or binge-watching.

Here's the funny thing, though: I've also been accused by many colleagues of being the most upbeat futurist they've ever met, especially given my work focuses on so many dark futures. I try to explain to them that it's my job to explore these threats but also make sure they don't happen. I'm actively making the future safer, and that keeps me from getting pessimistic about tomorrow.

The Thing That Does Scare Me

Being the futurist who invented threatcasting, one who spends a fair amount of time exploring dark places, I am often asked what scares me the most. I've been getting this question for years. When it comes from a reporter or TV talking head, I usually reply that what really scares me is when people give away the power they have to build their own future. Which is true. When people give up their ability to imagine and build their future, nothing good comes of this.

But that's not the whole story.

Recently, a dark future has emerged that truly frightens me. In 2019, my lab looked into a specific kind of future threat: the undermining of truth by technology. Specifically, we looked at disinformation (speaking facts that aren't true), misinformation (sharing untrue facts without the knowledge that they are not true), and malinformation (sharing personal or damaging information about a person or organization to harm them). All three are looped into what the Council of Europe defines as "information disorder."

At the Threatcasting Lab we looked at the effects of information disorder ten years out, when it might be enabled by a constellation of new technology advancements. Our main findings were this:

> In the coming decade, advances in technologies like artificial intelligence (AI), machine learning (ML), quantum computing, the internet of things (IoT), smart cities, and autonomous vehicles in land, sea, and air will enable adversaries of the United States to mechanize information disorder to influence, manipulate, and harm organizations and individuals. These coming information disorder machines (IDMs) will be targeted broadly at groups and geographies. AI and ML will allow for increased if not complete automation, allowing IDMs to adapt in real time down to the individual level, creating personalized attacks while operating at a mass scale. The emerging threat of IDMs lies in the unique pairing of their real-time microtargeting and the macro effects that can have at scale. This is a direct threat to national and global security as well as a threat to the future of the United States of America.[*]

Like I said, not for the faint of heart. Basically, what our threatcasting found was that in the not-so-distant future, ene-

---

[*] B. Johnson, "Information Disorder Machines: Weaponizing Narrative and the Future of the United States of America," Arizona State University, 2019, http://threatcasting .com/wp-content/uploads/2019/10/threatcasting-2019-w-footnotes-PRINT.pdf.

mies, criminals, corporations, and just about anyone will be able to target you as an individual and create information, news, and stories tailored to you. This information could be not true at all or only slightly true, but it will be designed to get you to do something you wouldn't normally do. Information "disorderists" will inflame your moral outrage, strike at the very things you hold sacred. They will continue to manipulate us to move against ourselves, tapping into racial, political, and cultural rifts in the US, getting us to fight with one another. These bad actors won't care if you're a Democrat, Republican, or neither. They won't care whether you're pro or anti on any subject whatsoever. They will simply use the things that divide us to divide us more, until we are fighting one another tooth and nail, enabling them to gain the advantage.

It's a dark future, but even the notion of information disorder tearing us apart isn't what scares me most. The thing that scares me is that even when we know it's happening, we won't do anything to stop it. It frightens me when people see a negative future coming and not only don't do anything to stop it but let it happen. They run toward it, even, pushing it on other people. It's this carelessness and this cruelty that frighten me. A world where people do this to one another is my dark place.

So how do I find the light? One of my inspirations is Carl Sagan, author, astronomer, cosmologist, astrophysicist, astrobiologist, and all-round explainer of scientific concepts. He famously said that, as humans, we have to understand that in the great drama of the universe, we are not the central actors. We live on a small blue rock that isn't even at the center of the universe. On Earth, we really just live in the suburbs of this vast and awe-inspiring universe.*

All we have in this enormous dark emptiness is one another. We can't be so careless and cruel. That's what I do when I go to my dark place. I realize that all we have is one another. That's why I wrote this book. It's how I deal with my own existential fears. I do it person by person, class by class, speech by speech.

How can you apply the process to your own dark places? Let me introduce you to a guy named Will.

Not Your Average Party Conversation

Summer was on its way to the Pacific Northwest. The months of rain and clouds had finally given way to crisp, clear skies, the chill in the air replaced by the steady warmth of the coming season. It was a Saturday, and we were at a friend's birthday party. There was the usual food, music, and banter, with a round of karaoke to come. My friends are serious about karaoke. I won't get into the details, but let's just say multiple costume changes are routine, along with plenty of pre-party rehearsals. "Bohemian Rhapsody" anybody? "Dancing Queen"? I'm not very good at karaoke.

---

*Carl Sagan, *The Demon Haunted World* (New York: Random House, 1996).

I've known this group of people for nearly twenty years. We don't talk about work at all. Most of the conversations center around sports, kids, and the latest gossip. That's why I was surprised when Will pulled me aside. "Can I talk to you outside?" he asked in a hushed yet urgent tone that was far too serious for a Saturday night soirée.

"Sure." I nodded, following him through the crowd and out onto the empty patio.

Will and I had met about eighteen years prior. He was the husband of my wife's friend, and over the years we had forged a close relationship. He grew up outside of Twin Falls, Idaho, on a working farm. Being a small-town boy myself, I enjoyed hearing stories about the rustic idyll—cow milking, calf birthing, and the like. As an adult, he'd spent his career in the big city, working jobs in human resources and upper management, but he'd never lost his rural roots. He still wore cowboy boots and didn't mince words.

Once we were outside, the party noise reduced to a dull murmur, he said, "I'm sorry to do this during the party, but . . ." He looked down at his boots, then up at me with a dark, hollow expression.

"What's up?" I said a tad anxiously. I knew Will well enough to realize something was wrong.

"Look, well, recently I've been feeling really worried, and you know, you're the futurist and all, so I thought I could maybe talk with you."

"Sure." I shrugged. "What's up?"

"Really?" he said. He seemed surprised that I would want to talk. "Great. I really appreciate it. But it's not the kind of conversation for here." He nodded toward the party. "Do you have time next week?"

"Sure," I replied. At the time, I had already made the move to our weekend place on the north coast for the rest of the summer. "Want to come out to the coast? We can talk there."

"Yeah, I can do that." Will nodded.

"It's a good place to talk," I added. "But are you okay for now? Are you sure you want to wait?"

"Yeah," Will said, making his way back inside. "It's not about Amanda and the kids or anything. They're good. I don't mean to worry you. It's something else. I'll explain more next week."

"Okay," I said, putting my hand on his shoulder. I could feel the tension. "What are you going to sing tonight?" I added, trying to lighten the mood.

"Johnny Cash," he answered definitively.

The World's End

The north coast of Oregon is formidable and breathtaking. Fifteen million years ago there was some serious volcanic activity on the border of Oregon and Washington. The lava spewed, flowing freely to the Columbia River basin, forcing out the water and increasing the coastline by some forty miles. Today, the coastal mountain range comes crashing into the cold waters of the Pacific Ocean.

The mountains and hills are lush with spruce hemlock and towering Douglas-firs. When the winter storms come, their evergreen branches roll and sway in the stiff winds, making the forest look like a tumultuous emerald sea.

The stretch of beach where I live is wide and flat. Because of the storms and the rough Pacific, the sand is punctuated by ten- to thirty-foot tree trunks that have washed ashore. Stripped of their needles and roots, they look like pale, hulking skeletons. The volcanic flow and basalt rock made Haystack Rock and the Needles, rocks that push up and out of the churning ocean like craggy spires that were once a part of the Coast Range, but have since been eroded, broken apart, and claimed by the mighty Pacific. To the north you can see Tillamook Rock Lighthouse, known as "Terrible Tilly." Locals like to say that if you can make out Tilly, the weather will be good that day. For most of the winter, Tilly is nowhere to be seen.

We call our house The World's End, because it's perched at the edge of the land, overlooking the ocean. The name feels especially appropriate when the winter storms roll in and the fierce winds make the house creak and groan, like a large, listing ship.

This small coastal community has a special magic that you have to experience to fully understand and appreciate. It's as good a place as any to take a stroll and talk about the future.

Will arrived early. I heard his truck pull into the driveway and the clomp of his boots climbing up the stairs of the deck. The door was open, so he came walking in.

"BDJ?" he called out.

"Yep," I replied, coming down from the loft to meet him. "How was the drive over the passes?" This is the usual question to new arrivals. In the winter you ask because of the ice and snow. In summer you ask because the views are so sublime.

"Beautiful," Will replied. "There wasn't anyone on the road."

We chatted for a bit about family life, though I could tell Will was eager to get to the topic at hand. He didn't know how to get started. My friends don't usually talk about these kinds of things with me. And guys like Will usually don't go there at all.

"It's a gorgeous day," I said, motioning to the ocean. The sky was pure blue, and there wasn't much wind. "How about we take a walk down to the beach?"

"That sounds good." He nodded.

The tide was rolling in, but there was still plenty of room on the shore. Our beach isn't known for big crowds, even in the summer. This being a weekday, it was nearly empty.

"What's going on?" I prodded Will. "How can I help?"

"Well, if any of this gets too weird or I sound like I'm crazy, just tell me and I'll shut up," he stated as we walked. "I've always been a little prone to worry. Growing up on a farm, you're always one cold snap or insect swarm away from ruin, so I guess it's in my blood. But lately it's gotten so much worse."

Unfortunately, the kind of anxiety Will was describing has become more and more prevalent in modern culture, especially following COVID-19. Even before the pandemic, there were more

than forty five million adults suffering from some kind of disorder, according to the National Alliance on Mental Illness. I'm not
a psychiatrist, but even in my work in futurism I've seen a decided
uptick in feelings of apprehension and dread.

"What are you worried about exactly?" I asked.

"Everything, it seems. I feel like a cliché, but you flick on the
news these days and it feels like one holy mess after another—
war, pandemic, wildfires, I mean pick your poison." He kicked
his boot into the sand. "It's not that I'm depressed. It's bigger than
that. It gets into my head and I can't stop thinking about it. It's
hard to concentrate on work. Sometimes I forget the kids are in
the room. Do you know how scary that is? It's like I'm losing my
mind."

"Say more," I probed.

"I used to have this recurring nightmare when I was a kid," he
started. "You and I are both products of the Cold War, so I'm sure
you can relate. Basically, in the dream, the world is on the verge
of nuclear war. I'm not just a passive observer. I'm a soldier in the
missile silo about to launch a warhead, bringing about the world's
destruction. And there's absolutely nothing I can do to stop it. It's
this combination of absolute powerlessness and absolute annihilation. I'm watching the world fall apart. That's kind of how I feel
all the time. Only there's no waking up from the feeling."

"Wow," I said. "That's really intense. Thank you for sharing
that."

"Hell," he said, raising his voice, "who cares about sharing? All the talking in the world can't help this. I feel like I'm losing my mind." His voice cracked and he swallowed hard.

I placed my hand on Will's shoulder, thinking if I could establish a physical connection with him that might draw him out of his state. He swatted my arm away with a force and suddenness that left us both a bit startled.

"I'm sorry!" He jumped away from me like he had been hit with an electric shock. Standing in the sand, he had the same hollow look in his eyes from the party, an expression of fear and powerlessness, all at the edge of an immense darkness. "What do I do, man?"

I needed to calm things down.

"Are you okay?" I held my hands up in front of me and didn't move. "We can go back to the house if you want."

"Aw hell," Will breathed. "I'm sorry, BDJ . . . I didn't mean to . . . Hell, everything is so messed up . . ."

I thought I could help. "The first step is to write down the future you want and the future you want to avoid," I started, following my usual script. "I know that might sound a little simple, but it can really help. It has power. In your case, I think we should just start with the future you want to avoid."

"Okay," Will said, glancing at me sideways.

"So what's the future you want to avoid?" I asked him.

"Uh, I just told you," he answered, with a hint of exasperation.

"Okay, yes, I get that," I said. "But a big part of my futurecasting process is being as specific as possible."

"I don't know how to be more specific," he said, a little frustrated. "No World War III? No nuclear devastation? No death. I don't want things to fall apart."

"That's a good start," I urged.

I could work with this. There's a process in therapy called the "catastrophe interview." It's used when the fears of the patient are dark and nebulous. The idea is to get them thinking about their current fears, then ask them what worries them about this future. What could happen in this future that makes them want to avoid it? When they answer that as concretely as possible, then ask them again: What's worrisome about this future? What could happen in this future that makes it so bad? When they come up with a concrete answer, ask the questions again. Keep doing this until they can't answer them anymore. That's when they'll know they've reached the very bottom of their worries or the future they want to avoid, when there are no more answers. This kind of self-interrogation or interview can be really helpful.

I started it with Will.

"What worries you about this future?" I asked. "What could happen in this future that makes you want to avoid it?"

"Well, the idea of war is awful," he said. I could tell he still thought I was crazy or maybe even poking fun at him.

"I know it sounds like a simple question," I explained. "But try to be as specific as possible. Apply it to yourself and your family."

"Okay," he said, looking out over the ocean for a long moment. "The chaos and uncertainty. The thought of war or famine or disease coming here and my wife and kids experiencing any kind of suffering."

"What worries you about this future?" I asked. "What could happen in this future that makes you want to avoid it?"

"War puts everyone at risk," he said. "A pandemic threatens the entire population."

"What worries you about that?" I asked.

"We'd be attacked," he said. "I could get killed. Amanda and the kids could die."

"What worries you there?" I asked.

"Death, man, my inability to stop it!" he shouted, kicking at the sand. "What if I can't stop them from getting killed? What if I die and leave them alone and abandoned?"

"That's pretty horrible," I said after a moment. Will had reached the bottom of the future he wanted to avoid.

"It's scary as hell, man," he said finally.

The Futurist Who Lives at the Edge of Death

The fear of death is normal and also incredibly powerful. It goes without saying that humans are afraid of death. But that's not good enough for me. My goal as an applied futurist is to give people new ways of looking at the future. I want people to see themselves in a different future, and empower them to avoid the darkness. Because of this, I've spent a lot of time talking to people about these dark places and what they can do about them.

Following the process, I've sought out experts who can give people a new framework for thinking about the futures they want to avoid. Even in the face of death, people are not powerless. I learned this from Richard Sear, a futurist who lives at the edge of death.

"I was on a flight from San Francisco to San Antonio and I had an attack," Richard explained to me one night over dinner. "They had to do an emergency landing in El Paso. I thought I was going to die for sure this time. I thought I was done for."

Richard is probably the most successful futurist you've never heard of. He's spent his career consulting for large multinational corporations and governments. He travels the world even more than I do, and if you've gotten this far in the book, you know that's quite a lot. You haven't heard about Richard's work because most of it is strictly confidential. He's helping these massive organizations plan for their futures, ten, twenty, and thirty years out.

Richard grew up in England and is a trained economist from the University of Cambridge. He has spent most of his career living in Texas, so he speaks in a proper English accent with a heavy Texas twang. He sounds like no other person I've ever met.

A few years ago, Richard started having these mysterious attacks. They were so severe that he would end up unconscious in the emergency room. I remember the days before his diagnosis. It was so frightening because he never knew when an attack would strike.

Richard travels so much that attacks would often happen when he was away from home or even out of the country.

Finally the doctors figured it out. He was suffering from a rare disease called severe idiopathic systemic mastocytosis, in which mast cells accumulate in internal tissues and organs, like the liver, spleen, bone marrow, and small intestine.

"An attack can happen at any time," Richard told me, "so I always travel with multiple EpiPens and histamine blockers. But the fact of the matter is, I could die at any moment. I know that sounds nuts, but it's true. There's no other way to explain it."

"What happened on the flight?" I asked.

"I knew something was wrong because when I'm going to have an attack my hands start to swell," he said, holding up his right hand. "My wedding ring starts to get tight. Immediately, I took a massive dose of antihistamine. I kept it to myself. I didn't want to get anyone worried."

"That didn't work?" I asked.

"Not at all, fella," Richard said. "I knew I had to get more serious, so I went into the bathroom on the airplane and injected myself with my first dose of the EpiPen. When I got back to my seat I knew we were in for a big one. I called the flight attendant and told him what was happening, so he could alert the pilots. Luckily there was a doctor onboard who knew about my disease."

"What a nightmare," I said.

"Yeah, it was a bad one, but I'd been there before," he said.

I was struck by how calmly Richard was talking about the incident—the attack, the emergency landing, almost dying. When he spoke, he sounded matter-of-fact, if not a little annoyed.

"What happened then?" I asked.

"I don't really remember much," he said, finishing his story. "The doctor gave me another injection of the EpiPen, and it was about that time that I lost consciousness. The next thing I remember was waking up in the hospital."

We continued with our dinner. Once the shock of the story wore off, I got to thinking that Richard was a futurist who lived with death every day of his life. The threat of death loomed over him constantly. So what did that mean to a futurist, to a person paid to think about the future?

"How do you deal with it?" I asked him. "As a futurist, how do you think about your future?"

"Fear is a wild thing," he replied. "That kind of fear of death can change you. It changed me. It makes you do things you wouldn't normally do. You can get really dark, if you let yourself."

"What do you do?" I said, leaning in. "You've lived with this for a while now. You're not dark. You're not pessimistic about your future."

"You take control," Richard said flatly. "You realize that even at the point of death you still have control."

"How so?" I asked.

"When I was on that flight, when I was sure I was going to die, just before I lost consciousness, I knew what to do. I pushed everything out of my mind. I pushed out the fear and the panic and, if I'm being honest, the annoyance. I was just pissed off, man." He chuckled. "If I was going to die, I was going to take control. I pulled an image up in my head. I have a picture on my bathroom mirror, a picture of my kids. I held that picture in my mind. An image of something that I purely love the most in life."

"That's how you gain control," I said.

"You just need that image, something to focus on," he said, pointing at his temple. "Even in the darkness, that is all you see."

I didn't know what to say. I was struck by the strength of my friend and the stark bleakness of the situation.

"Thank you for telling me this" was all I could get out.

"No problem," Richard continued. "Don't get too dark about it. You know what? I actually don't want my condition to go away. I wouldn't want to stop living like this."

"What do you mean?" I said, not following.

"I'm a better person because of it," he answered. "Truly a better person. I'm a better husband and a better father. It's brought me much closer to my faith. I wouldn't change it."

This was an enormous revelation. Even at the edge of death, we can have power. We can focus on the things we love most in life. Even if you're going to die, you can decide what you see in your mind.

But this was just the beginning of my conversations about death and dark futures. Only a short time after my dinner with

Richard, I met up with a former student of mine who revealed her own fixation on death.

The Futurist Who Stares into the Abyss

Julia Rose West is a successful Silicon Valley futurist. She was a student of mine years ago, so I'm abundantly proud of her success and, yes, a little biased too. Julia works with research teams to design future products and help companies prepare for the future. What many people don't know is that before Julia decided to be a futurist she was a professional barrel racer in the rodeo.

We met up in an upscale Mexican restaurant in San Francisco. It was at the end of the workday so the room was abuzz with chatter. We found a quiet spot tucked in the back to chat.

"My job as a futurist is not to make predictions," Julia began. "I spent enough hours in your classroom to know that. My job is to help companies and people prepare for the future. But there is one thing that as a futurist I can guarantee you with one hundred percent certainty, and that is that you are going to die."

"So how do you help people prepare for that?" I asked. "As someone who thinks about the future and prepares people for it, what do you tell them?"

"I start by saying that I care deeply about what that unknown future might do to you personally or your family and loved ones.

It's scary. But if you really think about it and ask yourself the hard question 'What's the worst that can happen?' it starts to put it into perspective."

"Therapists use a similar approach," I agreed.

"If you take a big problem that's stressing you out and ask 'What is the worst that can happen?' the answers are usually similar—job loss, divorce, homelessness—and sometimes the answer is even worse, including death."

"For many people it leads to that," I said.

"Well then," Julia said, rubbing her hands together. "Death is something to consider. So let's consider it. What happens if you die? You entered into this life knowing that you will die. Whether or not you like to think about it, or admit it, it is a fact. You will die. It is something every human will not escape. You will die. It is just a matter of how and when."

"It's an overwhelming fear for most people," I said. "They don't know where to start."

"When you think about overwhelming fear, there's a way to deal with it," Julia said. "Let's take the fear of flying. How could you think through that? If you're faced with a fearful future where death is one of the possibilities, ask yourself these two things: 'What is the worst that can happen?' and 'What control do I have over it?'"

"Makes sense," I said.

"To use the example of flying, you are not the pilot, you don't have control over the plane. But you do have control over your emotions during the flight and possibly, if this is the way things unfold, the way you handle your death. I like to think of it as death with mental dignity."

"I was just talking with another futurist who had a similar view," I said, mentioning Richard. "He says that you have control over the last thing you see."

"And that gives you control over how you handle it," she affirmed. "You take back control and don't worry about the rest. Also, it's important to realize that the reason you have fear about leaving this life *only* exists because you have experienced some really great things. Hold on to those experiences. You are incredibly fortunate. That moment of fear, that worry about death, can't hold a candle to all the experiences in your life."

"That's a great way to reframe the fear," I replied. "The reason you are feeling any fear or these dark futures is an affirmation of your life. Thinking about that life pulls you back from the fear. It gives you your power back."

"Think about the future and acknowledge all the possible futures," Julia said. "Include those darker fears. You can become more resilient to the surprising futures that may come your way. And trust me, you will have to deal with your fair share of challenges, like death and illness. But in the process, you will learn to value your present, the life you have now, and not sweat the small stuff, therefore reducing the risk of unfavorable futures. By focusing on the future, you can become more present in today and live a richer life."

It was striking to me how two futurists ended up with the same advice but came at it from different paths. The insight was clear. When you're thinking about dark futures that feel overwhelming, the first step is to accept the fear. Explore what the worst thing is that could happen. Then find your power. Ask yourself what you have control over. And recognize what you don't have control over. As Julia said, if you're not the pilot, you don't have control over the plane. Recognizing what you do have control over gives you something to focus on and something to do.

In the very extreme, like with Richard, you have control over what you see. And like Julia said, you can meet death with mental dignity.

All Your Dark Tomorrows

As Will and I continued down the beach, I recalled my exchanges with Richard and Julia. "It's good that you're scared," I said. "It's good that you recognize it and are talking to me."

"It doesn't feel that way," Will demurred.

"Fear of death and catastrophic events like pandemic and war are tricky," I answered. "It's good to recognize that part of the power of these fears comes from your love and caring for Amanda and the kids. That's the fuel. You're worried about losing them."

"For sure," Will said quickly. "I know that."

"But let me ask, are you connecting with them right now? How much are you living in the present? Don't let an existential fear of the future take away from your today. The more you worry about these big fears, the more it should push you to value what you have today. That can help lessen the fear and make it more manageable."

"How do you know all this?" Will asked.

"Working in this field, I have a lot of friends and we take this seriously," I said. "We talk about these things and what we can do to help. When it comes to these fears, value the bright today more than the dark tomorrow. Now, if the dark thoughts grow into something more unhealthy, you'll need to seek the help of a professional. I'm not qualified for that. I can help with the future, but not mental health."

"Gotcha." Will nodded. "I'm good. I don't think I'm clinically depressed. I've just been in my head more than normal lately."

Sometimes when people are worried about big existential fears it's not really that fear that's eating at them. That's why these dark futures can be so tricky. It's usually about power, and it's usually personal.

In the first few decades of the twenty-first century we've seen an uptick in depression, addiction, and suicide in middle-aged white men, guys like Will. According to the Centers for Disease Control and Prevention, in 2017 life expectancy fell for the second time in three years. This has mainly been driven by a surge in opioid overdoses and suicide in white men. That's why it's so important to recognize the fear at its root and act on that.

"You need to understand the fear," I continued. "The next step is to ask yourself what you have control over and what you don't. If you're scared of flying, realize that unless you're the pilot, you don't have control of the plane. And you have to be good with that, good with understanding that you do still have control over your state of mind. You by yourself will not be able to prevent a war or stop the world from falling apart."

"But," Will started, then paused. He stopped walking altogether. We stood side by side on the sand, looking out at the small waves breaking across the Pacific. The conversation was heavy, but the sound of the surf was soothing. "How do you figure out what control you have? Take something big, like war or even an economic downturn. I get that I can't completely control it. But when I think about that, where do I even start?"

Threatcasting Away Common Fears

I take all of my work seriously, but especially when it relates to fear. Living scared is no way to live, so it literally pains me to see people trapped in that mindset. As serious as I am, there are times when a lighter touch is possible. Over the years, I've developed a kind of party trick that I like to call Beers for Fears. It usually busts out at gatherings with old friends, but I'll go there with relative strangers if the mood is right, maybe during a happy hour social at a conference.

The rules are pretty simple: someone names one of their biggest fears, then I lead the group in a spontaneous threatcasting exercise, showing the person a possible way out of their fearful state. I should stress that I'm always careful to differentiate between everyday fears and deep-seated phobias, the kind that require clinical treatment.

The game has revealed dozens of fears, some more unexpected than others: fear of in-laws, fear of cooking, fear of eye contact. The one that probably comes up the most in Beers for Fears is public speaking. I've come to realize that I'm a real freak in that I actually enjoy getting up in front of large crowds and talking off the cuff for hours at a time.

By some estimates, glossophobia, the technical term for the fear of public speaking, affects 75 percent of all adults. So what do I say when it comes up in Beers for Fears? It depends on the individual, but I always start with the same question: What kind of public speaker do you want to be? Some people want to address large crowds, while others just want to be able to give a toast at a dinner party. Once the future is defined, the group and I are off to the races, identifying the people who can help (friends and colleagues, often), available tools and resources (teleprompter software, support groups like Toastmasters), and experts in the field (including public speakers they admire). Within minutes, the person almost always feels like less of a glossophobe. In one very memorable round of Beers for Fears, our subject even stood up to say a few words. "I just want to say something," he began, looking around the room. "Thanks." That was it. And that was huge.

Lots of other good results have come out of Beers for Fears. If I ever bump into you in an airport lounge or hotel lobby, remind me to tell you about the dude who was afraid of snakes who was dating a zookeeper. It's a classic. And don't be shy about asking to play a game of Beers for Fears. As long as the first round's on you, I'm always game.

The Futurist Who Harnesses Nightmares

Alisha Bhagat is fascinated by complex systems and has devoted her career to learning how such systems work, assessing the problems therein and making them more manageable. She studied anthropology as an undergraduate at Carnegie Mellon and, after a few years in India and Sri Lanka, went on to get a master's in foreign service at Georgetown University. Working for the US government as a research analyst, she engaged with scenario models, assessing critical areas like radicalization, security in the Indian Ocean, and water resources in the Middle East. Throughout her career, she has focused on the immediate problems in human culture as well as worked toward creating positive long-term change.

Alisha is really good at solving complex problems. She has incredible insights into how individuals can find their power and take control in the face of overwhelming, existential problems. We chatted one afternoon by phone while I was in my library in the Pacific Northwest and she was working out of her office in New York City.

"I was just talking to a young student about existential angst," Alisha began. "She was telling me that she gets overwhelmed by climate change and its effects."

"That's a complex problem for sure," I said.

"The student didn't know what to do. Should she stop eating meat? Stop buying new clothes and partaking in overconsumption? She was fearful of the effects of climate change, and at the same time she felt guilty that she wasn't doing enough."

"Humans brains shift to fear in those moments," I said.

"Fear and guilt have an addictive quality, especially when they're paired together. People are worried about the catastrophic future, but they're also worried that they're messing up in their day-to-day lives."

"So what did you tell her?" I asked eagerly.

"Well, first I told her, 'You can't stop climate change by yourself and you need to understand that and be okay with it,'" Alisha answered. "Then I told her that she needs to understand what's in her control, what's in her power, and take action. If she messes up a little here and there, that's okay. Just pick yourself up and keep trying."

"But how could your student determine where she has control?" I asked.

"All of our power comes from the connections we have to the people around us," Alisha replied. "So you map the people around you. You might think you're powerless, but take a step back, look at the system, and ask yourself where you can have impact. You might assume that you have no impact, but look at where you sit in the system. Who are your people?"

"The future is built by people," I chimed in.

"Exactly," she agreed. "Map it out. Everyone lives in an eco-system of people connected to other people. You might not be connected to high-ranking policymakers, but you have local representatives, and these people do have connections to the decision makers."

"So it's not just about your people," I said. "It's also about how your people connect to other people, especially when we're talking about big issues."

"Yes," Alisha answered. "Those connections have power and impact. Start to work with your people to impact the people they have connections to. I know it sounds complex, and it's true these are big, tricky problems. But this is a way to get started, and you can really see that you are affecting the future you want to avoid."

The point reinforced a larger teaching of futurecasting, the idea that when tackling seemingly monumental tasks (i.e., changing the future), it's important to break the process into smaller, more manageable parts: baby steps.

I thought the conversation was winding down, but Alisha suddenly added, "We also have to talk about nightmares."

"For sure," I replied. "What about nightmares?"

"Why do we have them?" she started. "Nightmares are a kind of stress test for the brain. Your dreaming brain comes up with worst-case scenarios and forces you to figure them out. They can be scary in the extreme, but it helps to see nightmares as the mind's way of training and prepping us."

"Steeling us against possible dark futures," I added.

"We gain power from nightmares, just as we do from our fears," she explained. "When you have a nightmare or you find yourself in the middle of an existential worry about the future, step back and process that. Know that your brain is preparing you for that possible future."

"So fear doesn't make you weak," I said. "Fear actually makes you stronger against the things that you're worried about."

Alisha then turned the conversation to a process she found immensely interesting called "Swedish death cleaning." The idea is that when you reach a certain age and you're nearing death, you start cleaning and tidying up your life. The process is both metaphorical and literal. You start connecting with people and telling them how you really feel about them, but you also start cleaning up your material possessions. You clean out the storage shed and empty your closets. You get rid of the prom dress that, at eighty-five years of age, you'll definitely never wear again.

The main goal here is to not be a burden to your family and friends once you're gone. But Alisha thinks it goes beyond that, to a kind of clearing away of past baggage. It allows people to physically get their lives in order and gain some solace instead of feeling powerless at the end of their life.

"My grandparents actually did this without even knowing it," she told me. "They went through and cleaned up their lives as a way of dealing with that life. Having the conversation with the fear that you have then makes you stronger."

"Fascinating," I said. "And hugely effective too, I imagine."

"People don't like to let their minds dwell on dark futures," Alisha concluded. "But it's good to think through them. Don't get trapped in them, but don't shy away from them either. Harnessing the power of these dark futures can give you practical steps to overcome them."

Finding Power in the Shadow of the Overwhelming

"The futurecasting process can help," I told Will. "Now that you have a deep understanding of the future you want to avoid, you understand the worst-case scenario that could happen if you let it. To take control of this overwhelming future, you need to map out the people who can help you."

"Like average people in my life?" he asked.

"It starts with the people you have immediate access to," I answered. "But this isn't just about friends and families and colleagues. For these larger, darker futures, you need to explore who you have access to and who can have an impact. If your future fears are based on policies and legislation, that might mean reaching out to your mayor or local representative."

"That sounds pretty complicated," Will replied.

"It is!" I said, nudging him lightly as we started walking back down the beach toward the house. "But this is a complex problem. Part of the fuel for your worry is that it all feels too big for you to deal with. I think that's why you reached out to me in the first place."

"You're right," he agreed.

"This is how I would approach it," I continued, "how I approach any larger-than-life threats that come up. It's a systematic way to start picking apart large fears and dark futures so that you can take immediate action. Instead of shivering at the base of the overwhelming complexity, you can see the problem for what it is, explore who is involved in it, and start doing something about it. I think you'll find there is less fear then."

We walked for a while in silence. The seagulls swooped and hovered overhead, hoping for a discarded snack from us, but we had nothing to give.

"Okay." Will nodded. "I think I have an idea about who I can talk to and what actions I could take. At the very least, I have a place to start. Anything else?"

"Yes. You also need to research the experts who have taken on your problem before. You can learn from them, and it will help give your vision of the future more detail. Also, you need to look for tools and resources, like technology or policies that could help prevent the future you want to avoid. The internet is a big help here, but also look to local government."

"Gotcha." Will nodded again.

"Finally, you can start backcasting, figuring out how to make progress away from that future you don't want." I kept this part light since I could see this was a lot of information for Will to process, but also the subject matter can be really draining.

"I bet if I could make any kind of progress at all I'd start feeling better," he agreed.

"Halfway. Partway. Monday," I said. "What will show that you are halfway to your goal? Next, halve that and see what will get you partway there. And finally, what can you do right now, or Monday? Shaping the future starts with the here and now."

Will stopped and turned to the ocean. He looked down at his cowboy boots and kicked sand lightly back and forth between his feet. I waited. I had no idea what was going on in his head, but I hoped our stroll had helped lessen some of his fears.

"I think talking to you is my Monday," he said finally. "Understanding what I'm really afraid of and also coming to grips with what I don't have the power to change. It already feels like progress." His voice was still flat and pragmatic.

"That's great," I said, happy that I had helped.

"Yeah," Will said, starting to walk again. "Amanda will be happy. She already thought you were pretty smart, but this should seal the deal."

• • •

As Will pulled his car away from The World's End later that afternoon, I felt good that I'd given him something to work with. Like I always say, the process is the process. So the fact that he was on his journey was progress. But as the days went by, I couldn't shake the feeling that there was more advice to give to people whose futures were clouded by feelings of existential dread. How do you actually put one foot in front of the other when you're in that state? I didn't have a good answer. But I knew someone who might . . .

The Futurist Who Went into the Darkness and Came Back

"I've written a new book," Douglas Rushkoff said, bounding up to me at a conference in Portland, Oregon. "It's called *Present Shock*. It's an indictment of futurists and everything that you do." He paused for dramatic effect, looking at me with a sly, beaming grin. "Here, I brought you an advance copy. I want to know what you think."

"That's awesome," I replied, giving him a big hug. "I can't wait to read it! How are you, Doug?"

"I'm good," he said, and we spent the rest of the afternoon catching up. (Later that week, I read his book and liked it a lot, but that's another story.)

I've known Doug for some time now. He's an author and documentarian whom MIT named one of the world's ten most influential intellectuals. But when I think about Doug, I think of the fact that he is an agitator for all the right reasons. Doug cares about humans. So we get along.

In 2018, Doug was invited to give a talk to a group of financial managers. They offered him a speaking fee that was so high he couldn't say no.

He captured the entire experience in an article titled "Survival of the Richest: The Wealthy Are Plotting to Leave Us Behind." Doug wrote: "Last year, I got invited to a super-deluxe private resort to deliver a keynote speech to what I assumed would be a hundred or so investment bankers. It was by far the largest fee I had ever been offered for a talk—about half my annual professor's salary—all to deliver some insight on the subject of 'the future of technology.'"

But they didn't want to talk about technology, the rich and powerful wanted to talk about the end of the world:

> "Finally, the CEO of a brokerage house explained that he had nearly completed building his own underground bunker system and asked, 'How do I maintain authority over my security force after the event?'
>
> "The Event. That was their euphemism for the environmental collapse, social unrest, nuclear explosion, unstoppable virus, or Mr. Robot hack that takes everything down.
>
> "This single question occupied us for the rest of the hour . . . For all their wealth and power, they don't believe they can affect the future."*

---

* Douglas Rushkoff, "Survival of the Richest," Medium, July 5, 2018, https://onezero .medium.com/survival-of-the-richest-9ef6cddd0cc1.

So when I was thinking about the dark futures held by Will and others like him, Doug was one of the first people I wanted to talk with. I called him up early one morning. He was on his way out of the house in the suburbs to catch the commuter train into New York City.

"I'm mentoring a friend's son," Doug said under his breath as he walked from the house, saying goodbye to his family.

"You get those calls too?" I chirped.

"Oh, all the time, and I'm happy to take them." He laughed. Doug and I have a lot in common. We both believe in the power of humans. It's important as we think about and build futures that we always keep humans at the center.

"I want to talk to you as a futurist who has seen the darkness," I said, bringing up his experience with the one-percenter money managers and his article. "You met the people who have all the money in the world, and still they talked about the incredible darkness and their own fear of powerlessness. And you came back from it. So my question is, as a futurist, what advice would you give to people?"

"Well, to start off, I don't consider myself a futurist," Doug replied quickly. "I'm more of a presentist."

"A presentist?" I balked. This sounded like a dodge to me.

"Yeah a presentist," he continued. "I think people use futurism, or any kind of thinking about the future, as a way to avoid the problems of today. We talk about how the future is going to be great so that we don't have to recognize that the present is crappy.

[Note: he didn't say 'crappy.' Doug is a master at intellectual cursing.] For example, we can all sit around and talk about how solar and wind power are going to save the planet, but people usually do that because they don't want people to talk about how all the oil and coal that we are burning is fouling [again, he didn't say 'fouling'] up the environment. I trust people who are precarious. I get worried that futurism is a cop-out for not taking action in the present."

I saw Doug's point. People do use the promise of the future as a way to distract themselves from the present. Still, I don't take this to mean that we shouldn't, and can't, plan for a better future.

"Yes and no," I said, agreeing and disagreeing at the same time. "But if we are not doing that, if we are actually planning for the future, then you are a futurist. You do believe in that, right? Designing a future that is better for all people?"

"Well, yeah." Doug chuckled. "But I had to make my point."

"It's a good one," I said, supporting him. "But as a person who has spent most of his career trying to make our technological future more human, what would you tell people? Can you give them hope for these big, overwhelming, dark futures?"

"Well, sure," Doug replied softly. "By the way, I'm getting on the train now so I should be a little bit more quiet. This is not really a train conversation."

"I can still hear you," I urged him on.

"Well, first I would say, find where you have power," he began.

"Find that one place you have power in your professional life and take incremental action."

"How so?" I asked.

"Simple stuff," he continued. "But important stuff. Like ask yourself in your job or in your purchasing as a consumer, can you try to use services or buy products that are 10 percent less? Maybe it's 10 percent less using slave labor, or 10 percent less of a carbon footprint. Hell, even 10 percent more local. You don't have to change the world all at once, but you can do it by 10 percent. That's a start, right?"

"Sounds doable," I agreed.

"You have to find the little stuff," he continued. "Ten percent is accomplishable, but you have to hold yourself to it. The greatest thing about these existential threats is that they are so big. They can send you into this vicious cycle where all things are bad, everything compounds upon the other, each feeds the other, and you are left completely powerless."

"That is overwhelming," I said.

"But to me," Doug replied quickly, "the bigger and more overwhelming, the better."

"How do you mean?" I wasn't following, but I was fascinated to hear where he was going.

"The bigger the threat, the more dangerous and vicious the cycle, the more places you have as an individual to start chipping away at it," Doug explained. "There are so many more 10 percents that you can start to work on. I get excited the bigger the problem because there is a larger landscape to start taking action and taking back control."

"But what about the people who can't even do that?" I asked, thinking about all the people I've met with limited means, who don't have the ability to even make a 10 percent change. They need it to buy their medication or make their rent.

At that moment the line went dead. I was worried that Doug had slipped into a tunnel on his trip into NYC and that I would never hear his answer. But a minute later my phone rang.

"Hey, it's me," Doug said. "What would I tell people who don't have any power? Or who at least feel like they don't have power? Is that what you asked?"

"Yes!" I yelled.

"Well, first I would agree that poor people don't care about the future. They're too worried about the present. They don't have the luxury to think about the future. They're just looking for the six dollars to get a room for the night."

"Right," I agreed. "So if you don't know where you're going to get the six dollars for the night or the three hundred dollars to make your rent at the end of the month, how do we empower those people? What do we tell them to deal with these big threats?"

"First, I'd say to them, Are you standing up?" Doug replied.

"What?"

"Are you standing up?" Doug repeated. "If not, stand up and put your feet on the ground, shoulder width apart. If your physical body doesn't have the basic feeling of safety, then you won't be able to think clearly. Start with who you are in that moment. Stay with what is certain and what really is. From there you can increase your circle of purpose and start to identify what you have control over. It's that basic."

"I see," I said.

"Even if you have nothing, you can still be certain that you are in your body and that you are here," Doug explained. "Start with that. Then identify the closest future thing that you have control over."

"Like what?"

"Like finding that six dollars to get a room for the night," he fired back. "That is your future at that moment. Focus on that and nothing else. Solve that and then move to the next closest thing that you can have an effect on. Don't get lost in the noise. Don't let—"

The phone went dead again. I stared at the screen, hoping and waiting for the call back. It came.

"There's one more thing," Doug yelled. "Oh, I have to stop yelling on the train. But there is one more thing."

"What's that?" I asked.

"When we think about these existential threats, I really just have one last word of advice. If you find yourself in the depths of worry and despair over the things that you can't control, there is something you can do." He paused.

"What's that?" I asked eagerly.

"Volunteer at your kid's PTA." He laughed. "I'm serious. If

you're worried about these big fears that you don't have a lot of control over, well, then take control, get to know your community. The best antidote to this kind of fear is action. Take action, volunteer. If you don't have kids, then volunteer at your local library."

"Because the future is local," I echoed.

"Yes!" Doug exclaimed. "If you're really worried about the apocalypse, the main thing you should do is go outside and meet your neighbors. They are the ones who really matter and the ones who will really help you."

"I love it," I said.

"Gotta go, BDJ," Doug ended. "Let's talk again soon." The phone went dead, this time for good. My mind went back to my favorite quote from Doug's article about the dark futures he discussed with the mega rich. "Being human is not about individual survival or escape. It's a team sport. Whatever future humans have, it will be together."[*]

Cookie Delivery at the World's End

Out on the north coast, my wife and I have taken Doug's advice. Each summer and winter we bake multiple batches of cookies,

---

[*] Rushkoff, "Survival of the Richest," https://onezero.medium.com/survival-of-the-richest-9ef6cddd0cc1.

wrap them up, and deliver them to our neighbors. We walk the neighborhood, knocking on doors, chatting with neighbors, and delivering hand-baked treats.

This might sound trite, but trust me, it works. People like people. People like to get to know their neighbors. And people like cookies! (You can even find out their food allergies, and if you can give them something special, all the better.)

I know it's silly. But it really does work. Over the years we have really gotten to know our neighbors. We know which ones love to chat and gossip about the local town. We know who is an introvert and doesn't want to talk, but when your truck breaks down in the dead of winter, they'll show up with a jack and jumper cables to help out.

As I noted at the top of this chapter, fear is all around us, and it can rule your life if you let it. But antidotes to this fear are also everywhere, in the form of other people. I'll give the last word on this to Carl Sagan: "For small creatures such as we the vastness is bearable only through love."*

Up Next: Closing the Loop

When you started this book, the future was a nebulous void that you were blindly hurtling toward. Through the last seven chapters, it's

---

*Carl Sagan, *Contact* (New York: Pocket Books, 1997), 430.

hopefully taken shape, or at least it's become a definable entity that you have some control over. In chapter 8, I'll show you how to bring it all together and get started on your future you. Truth be told, you've been at it throughout the book, you just didn't realize it. That time is now. Let's go!

CHAPTER 8

Futuring Forward

have always found that the best way to prepare for the future is not to plan for it at all," Colonel Marcus Hammerland said bluntly.

"Why is that?" I asked.

We were walking on the grounds of the United States Military Academy in West Point, New York. I had been invited to be that year's speaker at the Castle Lecture. The next day I would address the entire incoming class about how to prepare for the future and what it will mean to be a soldier in the next decade. It was an incredible honor that capped off a few days of meetings, tours, cadet roundtables, and dinners. It was during a short break that Hammerland, my host, asked if I wanted to have a walk around the grounds.

"Well, you see, BDJ . . ." Hammerland continued, peering out over the Hudson River. His voice trailed off for a beat or two.

"I'm wondering what exactly you're going to say to the cadets—about the future, that is. I myself believe that a plan for the future isn't worth a damn."

Hammerland had spent his entire career in uniform. Before becoming a strategic planner and professor at the academy, he was a tanker, a fitting moniker for soldiers stationed in an armored division, where they deal primarily with—you guessed it—tanks.

This fact makes two things about the colonel completely understandable. First off, he's what you might describe as a fireplug—broad, stocky, strong. Though in my mind, calling him a fireplug didn't do justice at all to his physique. Hammerland made a fireplug look svelte. It was like he was built specifically to fit inside a cramped tank.

Then there was his voice. No matter what Hammerland was saying, it sounded like a direct order. I had worked with enough tankers to know this was a common trait, the result of less-than-perfect hearing from years inside a small metal box firing off large explosives. Saying the work is very, very loud is a spectacular understatement.

"Well, sir," I replied, "there's a difference between having a vision for your future and having a plan for that future."

"Don't call me sir, BDJ." He smiled. "You aren't in the Army. My name is Marcus."

"Yes, sir," I replied. "General Eisenhower had a great quote about plans and planning."

"'Plans are worthless, but planning is everything,'" Hammerland said, right on cue.

"That's the one," I said.

The quote came from a 1957 speech, which Eisenhower began, "I tell this story to illustrate the truth of the statement I heard long ago in the Army: Plans are worthless, but planning is everything. There is a very great distinction because when you are planning for an emergency you must start with this one thing: the very definition of 'emergency' is that it is unexpected, therefore it is not going to happen the way you are planning."*

"These young men and women need to understand that the future is complex," Hammerland continued. "They can't get caught thinking one thing is going to happen only to have another thing come along and catch them off guard. Does that make sense?"

"I understand what you're trying to get at," I replied. "But I think you can look at it differently. At least as a futurist I look at it in a different way."

"How's that?" he asked.

"You always have to have a vision of the future," I explained. "We know that nothing great ever happened that wasn't first

---

*Federal Register Division, National Archives and Records Service, and General Services Administration, *Public Papers of the Presidents of the United States: Dwight D. Eisenhower*, "Remarks at the National Defense Executive Reserve Conference, November 14, 1957" (Washington, DC: US Government Printing Office, 1958), 818, https://babel.hathitrust.org/cgi/pt?id=miua.4728417.1957.001&view=1up&seq=858.

imagined. That's true for the Army and it's true for regular civilian life. Seeing the future is essential to reaching your goal."

"I'm tracking you." Hammerland nodded.

"And if you can see your future, you can make a plan to get there. That's what I do with people and companies all the time."

"Yes, well, it's still the plan part that I disagree with," the colonel interjected.

"I get it," I said, pushing on. "But the plan is important because to get to it you have to do the planning. And planning is the act of looking into the future and figuring out what will get you there. The plan might change—"

"The plan will change!" Hammerland bellowed.

"Yes, the plan will change because our lives change. We're a dynamic species. And that's okay. It just means being in a constant state of reexamination. You need to keep planning. Everything will work out if you keep looking into the future and planning for it."

Hammerland nodded. "Because when things do change you'll be ready for it."

"It's more than that," I said. "If and when things change it won't be a big deal. Because you will already be adjusting, planning, moving forward. It will all feel normal."

The afternoon sun ducked behind a set of clouds, causing a sudden drop in temperature. Walking around West Point is awe-inspiring. It can scramble your brain, especially if you're a history buff. As Hammerland and I wandered the paths, I knew there was a good chance we were following in the footsteps of Eisenhower himself. George Washington walked this path. The thought made me a little dizzy.

"Isn't that one of your nutty West Coast sayings?" Hammerland said. "It's about the journey, not the destination." He was giving me a hard time, but his tone had softened.

"It's not my saying, sir," I said. "But yeah, I think it applies."

"I told you don't call me sir, BDJ. Call me Marcus."

"Yes, sir." I smiled.

"Come on," he said. "Let's head back to the house. I need to deliver you to a fancy dinner in under an hour."

Coming Full Circle

As the journey of this book comes to an end, I'm reminded of that conversation with the colonel, because it captures a final, crucial lesson of futurecasting: the process is not just a strategy, it's a way of life. Most people or companies or organizations come to me with a specific problem that needs solving (navigating a career change, leveraging some new innovation, preparing for globalization). My first task is to see them through that particular futurecast. But I don't consider the work finished until I've convinced them that they then need to start futurecasting the next challenge. Remember that great scene in the movie *Glengarry Glen Ross*, when Alec Baldwin schools his beaten-down sales force in the lessons of ABC, or "always be closing"? Well, for me, it's more like ABF: always be futurecasting. It truly is a lifestyle.

For so many people, the future feels like a blind spot, something they can't see and can't change. Futurecasting is a way to remove the blinders, once and for all. The process is so empowering because, through it, you learn that by starting *today* you can take the steps necessary to reshape *tomorrow*. After twenty-five years in the business, I know how excited people are to get started, once they see the clear steps of the process. But the real breakthrough comes when they see how the process can be applied again and again. It's like unlocking one of life's great secrets.

By reading this book, you're connecting to something bigger, while at the same time pulling back and seeing where things can go in the vastness, seeing all the possibilities. Ultimately, however, it comes down to everyday processes. The connection feels stronger because you now know what you need to do Monday, and Tuesday and Wednesday too, and that you can actually accomplish the things you want to accomplish.

My hope is that the future doesn't feel bigger than you anymore. It's no longer vast and scary, no longer a dark, unknowable abyss. You feel not only like you can create the future you hope for but like you will, as long as you continue to follow the process. The future isn't fixed. It's created, and re-created every single day, by people like me and by people like you.

To help drive this point home, I went back to some of the folks I introduced in this book to see how they were making out, and also to see what advice they would give to others just starting out on the futurecasting journey.

Why Futurecasting Is Like Cooking

I was lucky enough to reach Susan, the Chicago-based marketing executive from chapter 3 who used the futurecasting process to reshape her career. She was doing well, happy on her new path, helping women-led start-ups find their way to relevance and growth. I wanted to see how things were going for her and if she had found a way to weave futurecasting into her larger life.

It just so happened that Susan was going to be on the West Coast, so she offered to swing by for a visit. We walked from the house down to the ocean. It was late afternoon, the beach bright and flat, with an orange light shimmering across the waves, which created a thin line of froth as the waves lapped onto the sand. Seagulls shot across the sky, then took on a lazy glide before skimming across the open waters.

"Now that you've lived the process intensely, what do you think about it?" I asked Susan. "Has your vision for the future changed?"

"You know, BDJ," she began, "when I talk about the process, I often describe it to people like cooking."

"Cooking?" I said with surprise. "Interesting. You've never told me that."

"Yeah," she continued, sounding pleased. "It took me many years to figure out that cooking isn't about finding the best recipe for a given dish. It's about learning and developing techniques, gaining a familiarity with the tools, understanding how different flavors work together. It's important to discover what most pleases your individual palate."

"Go on," I said, curious to see where this would lead.

"Then, when you know how you like to cook, you can engage in larger conversations with other cooks who have also discovered their palates. It's an absolute joy to share your individual take on food with others. Nobody's recipes are the best. There is no 'right way' to cook. The joy is in the discovery and learning, alone in the kitchen and then sharing with your larger community of cooks."

"Let me make sure I understand you," I said. "Seeing yourself in your future, thinking like a futurist, is like thinking like a chef or a baker?"

"More cook than baker, I think," she said. "Baking is all about precision. Cooking leaves room for improvisation. When you're creating a dish, you have to imagine it first, just like a futurist."

"That makes sense," I said, starting to understand.

"And that's not all," Susan said excitedly. "The thing you do with people, BDJ, is give them tools and techniques, but you can't cook the dish for them. All cooks need to make their own dinner; each person needs to imagine and then build their own future."

"I totally agree," I said.

"You give people the tools and techniques and even sometimes the recipe," she said, "but I had to make the meal in my kitchen."

"I think you're exactly right," I said. "That's a good way to describe it."

"Just like chefs get joy from sharing with others," she continued, "no one person's future is right or better than another person's. Your future is right for you. But sharing how you got to that can be a joy."

"I think you can go even one step further," I added.

"What do you mean?" Susan asked.

"Many cooks love to teach," I said. "They especially like teaching family and friends." I paused to let the idea settle into my brain. "In the same way, now that you have learned the process, you can share it with other people. You can help them do the same."

"That's wonderful and joyous and I love it," Susan said with a smile, giving me a big hug on the beach.

Tech Check

A few weeks after my oceanside chat with Susan, my phone buzzed out of the blue one weekday afternoon. I was in the departure lounge at LAX, on layover to Australia, where I'd be working for the next few weeks, doing threatcasting with various government and military agencies. It was still a while until boarding, so I welcomed the distraction.

"Yo, BDJ," the text read. "It's your favorite pasta sauce. Got time for a chat?"

Alfredo! It had been more than a year since our drive into Denver. We'd exchanged a few texts here and there, but I was eager for an update.

"With extra cheese, please," I texted back. A few moments later, Al was on the line. After a bit of idle chitchat, I asked how his futurecasting was going.

"Yeah, that's what I really wanted to talk about," he said excitedly. "It's been transformative, truly. Instead of waiting for the doctors and medical staff to tell us about the next generation of CGM or insulin pump, we're totally on top of things."

"That must be empowering," I said.

"One hundred percent," he answered. "Then there are all the clinical trials, including some really exciting work with islet transplantation. It's one of the most promising pathways to a cure. You need to be eighteen years old to participate in the trials, so my boys are still too young, but it's something to look forward to."

"Do you feel like they're getting closer to a cure?" I asked.

"That's the funny thing," he said. "At the last conference I attended, someone in the audience of course asked that question. And sure enough, the answer was the same 'five years out' that I've been hearing ever since the boys were first diagnosed. But for some reason, it didn't trigger the same feelings of despair."

"I think that's because you're now an active participant in the future, rather than a passive bystander," I said. "You're no longer letting your future be controlled and determined by doctors and biotech firms."

"Yeah, it's really changed my entire lens on the future," he said. "One final update: I've tapped into this whole community of T1D parents who have figured out a way to hack into the insulin pump and CGM so that the two devices talk to each other, creating what's known as an 'artificial pancreas.' The manufacturers are all working on it too, but slowly. This community that I'm now a part of is really driving the innovation."

"Wow, that's very cool," I said. "How do your boys feel about it?"

"It's funny you ask," Al said. "Theo is all in. He'd start 'looping,' as they call the process, tomorrow if he could. But Jason is skeptical. In fact, he's actually gone in the opposite direction lately, taking breaks from the pump and CGM in favor of old-fashioned finger pricks and shots with the insulin pen."

Al was clearly befuddled by the different responses to technology from his two sons, but it made total sense to me. It reinforced the core truth that technology is merely a tool. It doesn't get to decide the future—humans do. Always have, always will.

"You know, Al," I said, "you're doing a great job helping your boys manage their diabetes. But even more than that, you're showing them how they're responsible for building their own futures, using whatever technologies are right for them. That lesson will last a lifetime."

"I thought you might say something like that," Al said. I could tell he was smiling on the other end of the line. I could also tell that futurecasting had become a way of life for him and his family, and that it was helping them navigate every new challenge.

"Hey, I got a flight to catch," I said. "Keep me posted on future developments?"

"Got you on speed dial," Al said.

We hung up, just as the gate attendant announced initial boarding for the flight to Sydney.

HERE WE GO . . .

Quick Questions 7

How are you feeling? Are you ready to start? Do you have your journal or device out? Are you starting to make lists?

This book and these stories are your toolbox, your cookbook. You have everything you need to get started. You can start envisioning the future you. You will discover the people, tools, and experts to propel you to the future, and you have the clarity of thought to chart out the steps that will get you there.

It's time to start.

QUESTION 1
What do you need to start?

I can't tell you your future. Now you have the ability to imagine and attain the future you. What's missing? What's holding you back? Reflect on specifics of the hardest part of futurecasting: overcoming your fear of the first step.

FOLLOW-UP QUESTIONS:

- **Where can you find what you need?**

- **What's standing in the way?**

QUESTION 2
Who are the people you should talk to?

You are going to build your future and people are going to help you, support you, and guide you. As you explore your future forces, writing down the people, tools, and experts that will propel you into the future you want—I have found that it's people that get you going. It's that one conversation you didn't expect. Go have a look back at Quick Questions 1 (chapter 2) and Quick Questions 3 (chapter 4). They can give you a starting place.

Next think about:

FOLLOW-UP QUESTIONS:

- **Where can you find that person?**
- **What is the one question you want them to answer?**
- **What is the one thing this person could tell you to get started?**

QUESTION 3
Did you know that you have already started?

You can do this because you've done it before. That's what we've been doing throughout this book. By reading this book you've already started moving toward the future you want.

Each exercise has given you a little more detail about the future you. Every story has given you examples for how other people have tried and applied the process. In fact, Quick Questions 2, the simplest of all the exercises in the book, was the one that contained every single step in the process. Review all seven exercises, do them again, deeply imagine the future you, and then you will have your start.

You are ready.

Ready for Liftoff

I hate missing flights.

In all my years of air travel, I can count the number of flights I've missed on one hand. I blame the ground transportation every time. Late car pickups, heavy traffic, no taxis when you need one the most—those snafus will bite you every time.

One time in New York I was trying to get from a robotics fair in the city to JFK International. The United Nations was in session, and to top it off, President Obama was scheduled to speak that day. My car had been late; traffic was at a standstill. I missed the flight by a solid hour. I like to tell people that Obama made me miss my flight, but it wasn't him. It was the ground transportation.

Bottom line: when I know it's going to be a race to catch a flight, I always have one eye on the clock and the other on the car status and traffic.

•••

"Who wants to know how to change the future?" I called out from the stage.

A roar of noise came from the audience. Some laughed, others clapped, many yelled, and some even raised their hands—so polite! I was finishing up a speech. I had three minutes to wrap up. We weren't going to take questions because I didn't have time. It killed me, but I needed to get to the airport. I had a plane to catch and not much time to do it. The flight would take me home, and I really wanted to get there. I'd been gone for almost two weeks.

"I can tell you," I called out, pacing back and forth like I normally do, energized by the crowd, even at the end of the show. "But you have to understand, you can't unlearn what I'm about to tell you. So I want to be sure here . . . Who wants to know how to change the future?"

A louder roar came back. Speaking in front of a crowd of seven thousand people is a funny thing. You don't really see the individuals. There are too many faces, and the stage lights make everyone dark. The mass of people looks like a gigantic wave pool at night. You know the artificial wave pools they have at water parks? Like that, but just after they have shut off the waves, and the water is splashing around, not in one direction but all over the place. The motion of the people moves in all directions, sometimes big rolling waves but sometimes little sneakier waves heading to the back doors to hit the bathrooms or answer their phones.

Two minutes left.

"Okay," I said, moving to the edge of the stage. "The way to change the future is to change the story you're telling about it."

The audience quieted down a little.

"If you can change the story you tell yourself about the future you will live in, you will make different decisions. I have seen it happen at large corporations and I've seen it happen with individual people. It sounds small, but it's a powerful thing."

I paused. One minute left.

"Here's my challenge to you," I said. "What is the future you want? Can you see yourself in it? Once you can, start to share that with your family, friends, and anyone who will listen. Through that simple act, not only will you see your future but you will change it and make it better. Thank you, everyone!"

The audience clapped, the music and lights came on, and I headed offstage, where Ron, my handler for the event, was waiting for me with my suitcase and coat.

"Right on time," Ron said, handing me my coat.

The stage manager gave me the thumbs-up. I waved back.

"This way," Ron said, leading me through the darkness backstage. It was a mess of cords, lights, and electrical gear. I knew to keep my head down and watch where I was walking. "The car is right outside, and traffic isn't too bad. It will be tight, but you can make it."

"I really appreciate all your help," I replied. "Tell everyone I'm really sorry I couldn't take questions. It's just the flight is so tight."

"Don't sweat it, BDJ," Ron said, pushing open the stage doors to a large hallway that led to the back door of the auditorium. I could still hear inside the theater the crowd chatting and the music pumping. A few stagehands were beginning to tear down the set.

Ron stopped abruptly. I bumped into his back. "Need a pit stop before hitting traffic?" he asked.

I did, but I had to make it quick.

For a backstage bathroom, it was huge. There were more than twenty urinals, though because it was backstage it was completely empty. Walking up to one of them, I glanced around and smiled. I remembered the times people had stopped me in the men's room after shows like this to ask a question. Good thing it was empty, with a flight to catch and traffic mounting.

"It's just down there," Ron said, pointing down a long hall to the exit. He passed me my roller bag and looked at his phone. "Yep, the driver is at the curb and you are good to go. I'm going to head back inside." He extended his hand. "It was good chatting with you, BDJ."

"Thanks, Ron," I replied. "Have a good time at that motorcycle rally with your lady."

"Count on it," he said and walked back to the stage.

I turned and headed for the exit.

I started doing the math in my head. The flight departed at 6:45 p.m. That meant they would start boarding at 6:15 p.m. I like to get to the airport at least an hour before, but I knew that wouldn't be possible. If traffic wasn't too heavy, if we didn't hit an accident or run into a sitting US president, I should be okay.

The car better be at the curb, my traveler intuition said reflexively.

I extended my arm to push open the door.

"BDJ," I heard someone call. "Excuse me, BDJ!"

I turned. The voice sounded young. Behind me, from out of nowhere, was a young girl. She couldn't have been more than ten or twelve. The sight of her stunned me. Was she lost and alone? No. I saw behind her what could only be her parents, looking on with pride and excitement.

"Excuse me, BDJ," she said, walking toward me. Clasped tightly in one hand was a book and a pen. It was one of my books.

"Yes?" I replied. "What can I do for you? I have a—"

"My name is Francis," she said, nervous but determined. "I read your book and really liked it and wanted to see if I could get you to sign it for me?" She held out the book and the pen.

The car is at the curb.

"Of course," I said, taking the book and signing it quickly. "Is that F-R-A-N-C-I-S?"

"Yes." She nodded. "But everyone calls me Franny."

Franny's parents approached and mouthed "Thank you" behind their daughter.

"I hope you enjoyed the book," I said, handing it back to her, impressed, since it really wasn't written for young folks her age. "Listen . . ." I started again.

The car is at the curb. The traffic is getting worse.

"Can I ask you a question?" she asked quickly, with a little more confidence. "I have a question about the future, and I think you can help. I'm only eleven, but I think it's important, and my mom says that maybe a futurist would know the answer, and you're a futurist."

I froze.

The car is at the curb. The traffic is getting worse. I am going to miss my flight.

"Okay, Franny," I said, parking my roller bag.

There is always a later flight to catch.

"How can I help?" I asked.

"Okay, futurist," she began, putting her hand on her hip and cocking her head to the side. "What I really want to know about the future is . . ."

ACKNOWLEDGMENTS

Thank you, Dan DiClerico, for your collaboration throughout this journey. Your insights helped me find the right structure and tone for the book with—as you said in our first meeting over coffee at the Roxy Hotel in New York—the all-important dash of magic. May we continue the stream of texts, emails, and video chats, along with the occasional martini or trip to Yankee Stadium. You are the best pitching coach a futurist could hope to have!

This book would have never happened without Leopoldo Gout, who said to me, "You know you should write a self-help book." To which I responded he was crazy. Turns out we were both right. If it hadn't been for his encouragement and support this book would not be in your hands.

Thank you to all *those* people . . . you know who you are. The people who posed questions; talked with me; asked for help; told me I was wrong; looked at me like I was crazy; shared their stories, hopes, and fears; took me into their confidence; and finally asked me personal questions in public places.

ACKNOWLEDGMENTS

My research home was an essential part of this project: Arizona State University's Center for Science and the Imagination, the School for the Future Innovation in Society, the Global Security Initiative, the Applied Research Lab, and the Threatcasting Lab.

Thank you to my team Ken Hertz, Teri Hertz, Jon Polk, Lisa Gallagher, Cyndi Coon, Gideon Weil (the Great Divining Rod), Sam Tatum, and Lora Keddie. As ever, thank you Mom and Dad. None of this would be possible without you both.

25.